I0152493

Ghost in the Desert

"The Apache Kid"

By

Zeke Crandall

This book is published by Zeke Crandall LLC.
6210 W. Shaw Butte Drive, Glendale Arizona
85304

All rights to this book in any form are strictly
prohibited unless authorized by the author.

The ISBN # 978-0-9773784-1-8
U.S. Copyright # TXu1-0-9773784-1-8
01/28/2009

For other books written by this author, including
Arizona Tales Vol 1, Arizona Train Robbers, The
Simple Man, The Power Affair, Canyon Diablo
and Pleasant Valley Revisited. Please contact the
author by email; zekecrandall46@hotmail.com or
our website; www.arizonatales.com or phone (602)
399-1811

Preface

The author was looking for an item on one of the online auctions when I came across an old Comic book for sale. It was one of the series about *"The Apache Kid."* I remembered the comic book series from when I was a boy. There was a whole series about *"The Apache Kid"* by Marvel Comics. The series ran from 1951 through 1971.

Below is a cover from one of the comics. The comic book series is definitely not politically correct by today's standards. I have a copy of this particular issue in my collection. It was released in 1957. The advertisements that were standard in comics for that time period are priceless.

The author regained new excitement the Apache Kid. I knew the real Apache Kid had nothing in common with the comic book hero. I obtained several copies of these comic books. I have become an avid collector of these comic books. The comic books have no bearing on the actual life of the Apache Kid but they do serve as proof that he was a forgotten character of the old west.

After reading some of these bizarre stories in the comic books, I started researching the story of the Apache Kid and discovered there were two movies that came out about this character. The first movie came out in 1941 and it was called *"The Apache Kid"* and starred a little known actor named Red Barber. I saw the movie one night on the old western television channel and it was nothing like the real character's life.

Then in 1957 some sixteen years later a second movie about the Apache Kid was released. The movie was called the *"Apache Warrior."* It starred Keith Larsen as the Apache Kid, Jim Davis played the part of a scout named and Eugena Paul played the part of the Apache Kid's wife in the movie. They tried to follow the Kid's life and the major events in his life but they were not very accurate in their portrayal of his amazing life. it was a low budget movie very typical for the 1950's.

Other inspirations for writing this story are the movie *"Walk the Proud Land"* which was released in 1953 and starred Audie Murphy, who played the part of John Clum. *"Apache,"* which is the story of the life of Messai. The film was released in 1954 and starred Burt Lancester as Messai. Then in 1968 came the movie *"They Stalking Moon,"* which was a movie about the Apache Indian Chief by the name of Salvai and starred Gregory Peck and then my favorite Apache movie was released in 1969 called simply *"Hombre,"* this movie starred Paul Newman as a white man raised by Apaches. Last but not least the movie *"Geronimo, An American Legend,"* starring Wes Studi as Geronimo. Gene Hackman played the part of General George Crook. Hackman is a very good likeness to Crook I might add. Last but not least the movie co starred Robert Duval who played the part of Al Sieber. The likeness of Duval and Al Sieber is uncanny. Hollywood casting experts do a very good job casting actors for parts.

It has been almost fifty years since anything has come out about the Apache Kid other than the great book written by Phyllis De Le Garza which was simply called *"The Apache Kid."*

In this book the author will present newspaper articles that follow the Kid's life well after most historians give up. It is impossible for any of us to know all of the facts about the Kid's life because it was so many years ago and the Native Americans in general do not keep written historical records. They pass down their history by word of mouth from generation to generation. The author will also present facts, photos and newspaper articles to validate this story of one of the worse outlaw and killer in Arizona History.

The Apache Kid is an old west character that has slipped through the cracks and has been forgotten for almost fifty years. It is time to bring him back to life for a new generation of Arizona history buffs. In this book the author brings back to life the Kid and tells the story of how we the white man, really took advantage of these Native Americans. Just like today, politics, power and money were the factors behind all of the hardships the Apache Indians suffered at that time.

The idea of the reservation system was a good one for sure but those initial Native Americans paid huge price so their ancestors today would be able to enjoy the privileges and rights of living on their own sovereign reservation nations but still are citizens of our great nation.

In a lot of ways their plight was no different than other conquered people in World History. The disrespect of others and greed have existed since the beginning of time. Sadly, though, this land belonged to all of the different Native American tribes, thousands of years before we ever heard of the New World, but again as we had to expand and build our Nation and these folks had to suffer the consequences of giving up their land but not without a fight in order to old the land and protect their way of life and consequently their very existence.

Chapter One

In this chapter the author will share a brief overview of the history of the Native Americans, who first settled in Arizona. The first people to arrive here in Arizona, was around 15,000 years ago. They came from a hunting culture that extended across the Great Plains and moved in seasonal migrations according to the food chain. Because they followed the food chain they built villages that were readily movable at the drop of a minute. Somewhere between 1300 and 1500, a tribe of this Athabaskan culture from west-central Canada arrived in Arizona. They were never a unified group, but they did follow the nomadic lifestyle of their predecessors. The group that stayed along the Colorado Plateau north of the Mogollon Rim became classified as *"Apaches de Navabu,"* and those to the south and east of the rim became the *"Apaches,"* after a Zuni word meaning *"Enemies."*

These two groups had tribal distinctions, but they shared a common trait, so the early Spanish named the land *"Apacheria."* Apacheria was the term used to designate the region inhabited by the Apache people. The earliest written records have Apacheria, as the region extending from north of the Arkansas River into, what are now the northern states of Mexico, and then from Central Texas through New Mexico west to Central Arizona. The Spanish refused to go north of Old Pueblo, know called Tucson for fear of the wrath of the Apaches.

The Apache adapted to this harsh country and became great hunters, fighters and survivors in the desolate hot, dry Sonoran Desert.

The Apache knew every mountain, spring, river and hideout in their land. The Navajo, *"Apaches de Navabu,"* settled the area north and east of Flagstaff above the Mogollon Rim. Their land covered what is now known as the four corners area which is the north eastern part of Arizona, the south western part of Utah, including the southwestern part of Colorado and the northwestern part of New Mexico. They still occupy this land today. They were farmers and ranchers, raising sheep and cattle. Their offspring still live there and still farm and ranch the same way as their ancestors. It wasn't until the early 1800's that the Apache and Navajo mortal enemies received the designations and land. The Navajo reside north of Flagstaff on the Mogollon Rim and the Apache occupy the land south of the rim in the southern deserts and to the east in the White Mountain area.

In 1736, a large silver strike drew thousands of Spaniards to an area in Southeastern Arizona Territory, called Arizonac. The name of the Territory was shortened around 1850 to Arizona, and when the Gadsen Purchase set the international boundary with Mexico in 1854. Through the 1840's most of visitors to our land just thought of it as deserted area to cross to get from California to the east and vice versa. The Indians were hostile, but not on the warpath.

Most of the Apache did not like the Anglos trespassing in their hunting grounds, but would tolerate it to a degree. The famous Chirachaua Apache Indian Chief, Cochise, still fuming over the fact that Mexico sold his land to the United States, even supplied them wood for their fires. He hoped that by helping them they would leave his land that much quicker. Cochise never could understand why he was not consulted at the signing of the Gadsen Purchase;

> *"What gave Mexico the right to sell Apache Land to anyone?"*

This was the big question in Cochise's mind his whole life that was never answered. Then in 1851 everything started to change in the territory.

The end of the California Gold Rush brought thousands of miners to Arizona on their way home to the east. They were broke, and tired of the lure of gold, so they headed home, but sadly most of them were broke by the time they reached Arizona.

By the mid-1850's, with the California Gold rush all but done, tens of thousands of prospectors turned their sights on Arizona, each determined to seek their fortune in the rich gold and silver fields. Farmers and ranchers followed, to cash in on the new booming market provided by the mining camps as well as Army posts sprung up everywhere. The Apaches revolted, and atrocities resulted on both sides, as each tried to drive the other out of the territory. With all of the influx of these folks the Apache became restless. There were interactions between the White settlers and the Native Apache. Atrocities occurred on both sides. But the army was going to do something to settle these disputes between the white settlers and the Apache.

In February 1861 the army set a trap for Cochise by inviting him to come to the table to discuss a treaty. He showed up unarmed along with his father in law Mangas Coloradas and another Chirachua chief, Nana. As soon as they appeared at army camp the soldiers surrounded them and opened fire. Mangas Coloradas was killed in the firefight but, Chiefs Nana and Cochise somehow, miraculously escaped alive from the battle.

With the murder of his father-in-law and more killings of his people, in late January 1863, Cochise went on the warpath. Geronimo, his closest childhood friend, who was not a chief but, was one of the most feared, respected warrior, hunter and tracker of the Chiricahua Apache people joined Cochise on the warpath. Geronimo went on to become one of the fiercest enemy in Arizona history. He and his band of renegades cost the American people a fortune, just hunting him as well as the loss of thousands of lives by his followers. There were a lot of reasons for his jumping on and off the reservation. The author will address Geronimo later in this book.

Cochise was very intelligent and used the distraction caused of the Civil War to invade and destroy whole towns and settlements. Nothing escaped his vengeance. At one point, he even burned to the ground the Mexican town of Tubac, south of Tucson. His war lasted twelve years.

A drawing of Cochise left, no pictures of Cochise have ever been found and Chief Mangas Coloradas is to the right.

During this time period on the warpath, he tortured his captives to death by slow fire, scalped and mutilated others, stealing women from the whites, Mexicans, making them slaves. The Apache believed that by torturing captive adults, they would take their power, so the longer and harder the captive went without dying the more power the Apache would obtain. The captive children that were spared, were raised as Apache or made slaves. By the end of the Civil War the whole Southwest was in such an uproar, that control of the hostile Apaches, proved to be the most serious threat in the Arizona Territory.

The Apache took every means possible to defend their lands from encroachment, and it was not long before they had a reputation as being the fiercest fighters in the entire Southwest. By 1870 the United States Government finally realized that a military solution by normal means was not going to work and that the only way to control the savages was to move them all to one place where rules could be enforced. The Government decided to round up all of the Apache tribes and place them on one reservations, and to teach them to farm and raise livestock. This program worked in other parts of the country and was very successful in Oklahoma with the Cherokee Nation.

After peace was established with Cochise in 1873. the army pushed on with the reservation system. What they forgot, or they conveniently ignored was that the Apache had traditional enemies among each of their own tribes from years of raiding each other to obtain food, horses, and captives, now they all were confined on the same piece of land. The situation was intolerable, and many warriors broke away from the reservation. The living conditions on the San Carlos Apache Reservation were good at first, and then the confinement, betrayal, floods, drought and disease took their toll on these nomadic people.

This story is based on the life of a great Army Scout and individual, who, because of a series incredible tragedies, became one of the most notorious killers and outlaws in the Arizona Territory. He was thrown into a situation that required a decision that would ultimately, have a tremendous effect on his life. No matter which choice he made it would be the wrong one. His story is no different than a lot of men that were outlaws in the old west, who became outlaws because of a tragedy or series of tragedies. The Apache Kid, was also known as *"The Ghost in the Desert,"* because of his ability to strike with the swiftness of a mountain lion, without warning and from anywhere both day or night, and who General George Crook called in his memoirs;

> *"The most ruthless, cold blooded, stealthily and intelligent Indian that ever lived."*

Most of us have been in no win situations. No matter what decision we made it would be the wrong one. We can only be thankful, that those decisions were not life or death decisions. There are many correlations of this with regard to outlaws in our time as well. Generally, there was a code in the Old West, unlike life as it is today.

Let us consider child molesters. They did not exist in the old west for more than one occurrence. They were either hung, castrated or found dead before they ever came to trial. Whether right or wrong, homosexuality was also not tolerated in the Old West, which is why the following statement for gay rights folks;

> *"they came out of the closet."*

There is no doubt that homosexuality existed. As the late great Senator Barry Goldwater was quoted;

> *"What's so knew here, these folks have been with us since the beginning of time."*

but they had to hide their lifestyles or suffer the consequences. Obviously this was a very archaic thought process that needed to be changed. Everyone knew who they were but as long as they kept to themselves they were not bothered. This was just the way it was in the Old West.

Below is a photo found in our National Archives of Cochise Stronghold in the Dragoon Mountains in Southeastern Arizona. One can see that once the Apache got to this place, with all the rugged rock formations, they were provided many hiding places. Also it must be noted that there was only one way in and one way out. Cochise Stronghold was simply a great natural fortress where they

Chapter Two

After guiding a group of readers on a historical tour of the Copper Basin, that includes Superior, Christmas, Hayden, Winkleman, Kearney, Miami and Globe in 1977, the author stopped at a local Globe saloon, on the way back home to have a cold beer. Globe is the largest town in the Copper Basin area and is just a little over a hundred miles south and east of the Phoenix on Arizona State Route 60.

I asked the bartender when he brought my beer if he had ever heard of the Apache Kid. He said he heard all about the Kid. Then he said yes and;

> *"it just so happens that the old medicine man at down at the end of the bar claims he knew the Kid."*

He suggested that I go down and meet the old medicine man. So, I moseyed on down to the end of the bar and introduced myself to the old man. He looked to be in his late eighties or early nineties. After the usual introductions the old guy smiled at me and said to me;

> *"I've been waiting for you. I said, Oh really!"*

Then he asked me if I was the one looking for information about the Apache Kid. He said he wanted to be sure that I was the one he was sent to meet. I just smiled and said;

"How did you know that I was in this exact bar at this exact time and would be looking for information about the "Apache Kid, but if he had information on the Kid, all was good."

The old man told me that he was blessed with the gift of seeing spirits, which is normally a gift which is generally bestowed to holy men, then he asked me if I would take him home so we could continue our conversation.

As we finished our beverages, I explained that I too had the gift of feeling the presence of spirits but nothing like him and that my youngest daughter could actually see them. My gift, as I laughed was probably due to the great LSD I dropped in the 1960s during the hippy movement. We left the saloon and headed east on Interstate 60, which is the main drive through Globe, until we were just about out of town. He instructed me to turn right into the Albertsons Grocery Store parking lot.

I grabbed a shopping cart and pushed it into the store following behind the old medicine man. Once in the store we went right to the produce department where he put a bag of five pounds of corn kernels, three oranges and a pouch of yeast in the cart. I asked him what he was doing. He told me we were going to brew some ceremonial Apache liquor called *"Tiswin."* He told me it would take five days for the new batch to be ready but that he had a fresh batch he brewed for this occasion a week ago.

During the drive from town to the old man man's home he spoke about his actual meeting with the *"Apache Kid."* He told me that in the summer of 1910 the Kid came to the San Carlos from his home in the Sierra Madre Mountains, in Mexico to attend a close childhood friend's funeral. After that and that they were raised in the same village. After the funeral he said;

> *"They all sat around a campfire and the Kid told all of the young braves present the story of his life."*

The old man said the Kid, went to the spirit world a little over a year later and that he died from what the coughing sickness, which we call Tuberculosis, at his home in Mexico with his family by his side. He told me the Kids family still live their today.

After talking about his initial meeting with the Kid he explained the steps to the brewing of *"Tiswin."* He said the kernels had to soak in the water for a day and then the husks had to be removed from each kernel and rinsed thoroughly. The five pounds of corn is then put in a crock pot or large container along with two gallons of water, six orange peels, two cinnamon sticks, one teaspoon of ground cloves and a teaspoon of yeast. Then the concoction is set in a warm place to ferment for five to seven days. He explained the Tiswin had to be kept cool and drank right away because it had no preservatives and it would turn to vinegar in forty- eight hours. The author told him that he had heard about Tiswin but never drank it.

We checked out at the cash register and the author paid for the items. Then we went due east on Interstate 60 toward Safford. Just inside the western boundary of the San Carlos Apache reservation he instructed me to turn right on the road that went south to San Carlos Lake. We drove about four miles and the author noticed a small subdivision of small tract homes on the west side of the road about a half mile from the road. We turned right just after we passed the first two homes he told me to pull into the next driveway which was his home.

It was a pretty ranch style home, light blue in color with a dark blue shingle roof with a front porch that extended from one end of the house to the other end. There were two wicker rocking chairs on the porch next to the front door that was in the middle of the porch. We grabbed the groceries from my truck and walked up to the front door. As the door opened he turned to me and said;

"Watch the first step because it is a real doosey."

The author followed him into the house and as I looked around he told me again to watch my step. The author looked down and there was a wooden fruit box inside the door to step down onto the ground. Once on the ground I looked around in amazement. The inside of the house was bare, no floors, no inside walls, no drywall.

There was a bed in front to the left and the right rear of the building appeared to be his kitchen because there was a refrigerator, sink, table, four chairs and an old pantry. Then right in the middle of the building was a wood burning fireplace. He walked over to a pile of wood stacked up on the right side of the front door, grabbed an armful of wood and threw the wood in the stove. He said it would warm up in a few minutes. At that point I was at a loss for words.

He told me that the homes were built for them about five years earlier and given to them by the Bureau of Indian Affairs. He said it was a cold winter and he used the floor and studs in the walls to keep warm that year and then as the years passed he tore down all of the interior drywall and stacked it outside then used the studs to heat him the next winters.

He went over to the refrigerator and pulled out a pitcher and poured the liquid into a couple of glasses. He asked the Gods to bless us and then we tapped our glasses with a toast before we started drinking the homemade concoction. He asked me what I thought of the brew. I told him it was interesting to say the least. It tasted like beer but had a better taste. It was kind of like an ale but tasted a lot smoother and definitely more potent.

As we drank the Tiswin the old chief dumped the corn into the sink and filled up the sink with water to soak the corn. Then he asked me to sit down with him at the table. The author told him the Tiswin was very tasty. He smiled and said it was very smooth considering it was about a 30 proof by volume concoction. Wow, I said, it won't take much of this to get a good buzz. The old medicine man laughed while he spoke;

"We are just getting started."

We finished two more glasses of the spirits and then he said it was time to get started. He went back over to the pantry and pulled out a plastic freezer bag that was full of tobacco. Then he grabbed a pipe, came back to join me at the table.

I looked at the tobacco as he walked back to the table. The tobacco had white dust all over it. He told me it was tobacco with peyote mixed in it. I said;

"In the 1960's during my college years, we ate the buds or made tea with them."

He told me typically that was normal but that he ground up some buds then let the grindings sit for a week in the sun then the were dry enough to grind into a powder that could be mixed with tobacco and make some killer tobacco. He said he could not handle the taste of the tea that is brewed with Tiswin and eating the buds was worse. It caused him major stomach aches and nausea. He went on to say that smoking the Peyote laced tobacco was a lot less toxic to the system.

Before he lit up the pipe with the pipe tobacco mix he explained what was going to happen so I could be prepared. He said we both had to shut our eyes and meditate. Once our minds were clear of all thoughts and enter the Black Zone or no thoughts we would be ready for him. At that point he said he would summon the spirit of the Apache Kid, who would reveal his life to our minds. He went on to say that sometimes the Kid appears in body form but most of the time it is a telekinesis thing with quick bursts of pictures. And sometimes he may not reveal himself to you but he will to me. He said it is hard to tell. It sounded completely bizarre but I had driven a long way and I have always had an open mind but no doubt I have also always been pretty naïve.

He filled the pipe with the tobacco and started to light up the pipe. Once it got hot he passed the pipe to me so I could take a drag. The substance smelled a little like tobacco but had a bitter aftertaste. Well after about six hits apiece we were both feeling no pain. I was familiar with Peyote having smoked it when I was in college in the 1960's and did remembered was it was a great high with no hangover so to speak.

I previously made plans to stay overnight there in Globe anyway but for sure I was in no shape to drive. I planned on getting a motel room for the night so if it got crazy I was covered. There was no way I was going to miss any of this amazing life experience. The old man asked me to meditate and clear my mind so the Kid could reveal himself. Soon I could sense someone else

- 20 -

in the room but I could not see him. The old man said;

"The Kid is with here us."

The Kid started to reveal his life, not saying a word, but in short flashing pictures to my mind. But the old medicine man was seeing the Kid's life from start to finish in complete pictures and the kid narrating his life to the old man's mind. The old medicine man then relayed the story to me.

I knew the Kid was there but he was not communicating with me. From this point on I will share everything the old medicine man relayed to me about the Kid's visit as it is burned into my memory banks. At this point I was just an observer, so I just listened as the old man, as the kid talked to him. At this point I was simply an observer.

Below is a picture of several plants as they grow in the wild. The buds are the only part of the plant that is harvested.

The Peyote plant grows only in southern Texas and all across the bordering States of Mexico. The largest area is in the Sierre Madre Mountains. It was used in religious ceremonies by the Yaqui and Mayan Indians in Mexico and the earliest use in America was by the Apaches and Navajo Indian Nations at in and around the late 1500s.

The information that was relayed to me was essential in guiding me in my research for this book. I have been able to verify most all of the facts and dates that were shared with the medicine man while I was present. I can remember seeing the Kid during that visit with the old medicine man like it was just yesterday. As accurately as possible from memory and research, I have recorded the Kid's story as told to the medicine man in my presence during that amazing visit. I can't even remember the old medicine man's name, but he assured me that I would remember everything. For sure these Native American folks are amazing.

After the visit with the medicine man, I know how the Native Americans pass down their history from generation to generation. He told me that certain people, usually medicine men or holy men know the person, who will carry the history for the next generation. We have historians that do this for our people, but their way is very special too.

At this point the author was lost. From time to time I would get a quick snapshot, like a picture of some boys playing and then from time to time other pictures would pop in my head but since I could not speak Apache, I was out to lunch. From then on the old man just interpreted and spoke for a good six hours. The crazy thing is that I to this day can still remember for the most part what he told me about the Kid's life. I can see how it would be so much more of intense, if I had been able to speak Apache but then again the old man said the Kid probably still would not have let me, you're not one of us. I am totally happy with what I learned on that visit with the old medicine man. Before I left though he admitted that he already knew most of the information, he shared with me.

Chapter Three

The Kid was born and raised in the village called *"Wheatfields,"* on the third full moon in the year of his ancestors 1861. Haska-bay-nay-ntayl, was his given Apache name, which means the tall one that will be a great leader. He said;

> *"Apaches named their children at birth with a name that most suited that child and usually from a unique physical character."*

He was also called Zeno-go-lache, the Apache meaning of this name is the crazy one. His father's was Toga-de-chuz and was the chief of their village. He relayed that his father and another Apache by the name of Rip sought his mother's hand in marriage. For some reason his mother chose his father over Rip. The reason was unbeknown to the Kid but his father was so elated at this turn of events that he could not resist belittling his rival before the rest of the tribe. This gloating contempt brought him a fierce enemy whose hate would endure for years.

The marriage between his father and mother quickly produced as son. The Kid's mother, Son-ju, was also the village healer. According to the Kid she was an amazing woman. She had been taught the skill of healing from her father, who was a great healer by his own right. He was the village medicine man. Sonju studied under his guidance as a young girl until she matured into a woman who learned all of her fathers healing skills.

The Kid's grandfather rode with Cochise until his death in early 1850. His mother told him that his grandfather was killed when he went along with Cochise to a piece talk with the Army in the Dragoon Mountains in Southern Arizona. She said;

> *"Cochise and her father went there to talk about the terms of a possible treaty. When they arrived they were surrounded by the soldiers and a firefight broke out. By the time reinforcements arrived at the scene, her father had been killed but saved the life of their chief, Cochise. She said he stayed and fought the soldiers single handed while Cochise and along with Chief Nana escaped, but stayed and fought until his death."*

Before his grandfather passed to the other world he shared all of his knowledge of finding herbs and healing remedies to his mother Sonju. She often took her young son with her out into the desert with her to help gather different healing herbs and roots. She explained to him about each herb they found and what illness the herb was used to cure.

The Kid learned everything he could about life and healing from his mother. The medicine man of their tribe was Captain Chiquito. The Kid's village was known as simply Captain Chiquito's village. They were one of the three villages of the Pinal Apache Nation.

"Wheatfields" was located about thirty-five miles north of present day Globe, Arizona on Arizona State Route 88. The village was situated just below a series of Anazai Cliff dwellings, now known as the Tonto National Monument that stood west of their village. Devil's Canyon marked the east boundary of their village. The village name came from the fact that it was surrounded by wheat and corn fields.

Below is a photo the Tonto National Monument taken by the author.

According to the medicine man;

"The Pinal Apache were farmers. They hunted and fished when they needed meat. According to the old medicine man, the Kid thought farming was hard work and long hours. He wanted to do something else to make a living. Farming was just not his cup of tea. Besides he longed for excitement."

By this time, the author was lost in thought and simply enjoying the visit. The medicine went on speaking from that time forward about the night he spent around the campfire with his friends and the Kid.

The medicine man said the Kid told him that every morning when he woke and stepped outside the family Wickieup he could not believe his eyes, when he looked up at the cliff dwellings, he said it was like he was seeing them again for the first time. They were simply majestic.

One can see from the picture below that was taken by the author that Devil's Canyon is located on the east side of their village was a natural fortress. It was virtually impossible to cross the Canyon. The only way into their village was from the north or south, which made their home easy to defend.

With the cliff dwellings on one side and Devils Canyon on the other side of the village, their village was easy to defend. When other tribes were seen approaching and danger was eminent, the people simply climbed up into the cliff dwellings. Once they were up in the cliff dwellings they pulled up the rope ladders and they were safe as it was impossible for anyone to attack them with any success.

There were four rope ladders that extended from the cliff dwellings first level to the floor of the valley. They were all about the same length which was about 100 feet long. The medicine man said that the Kid went on to say that the young braves were urged by their families not to visit the cliff dwellings because the spirits of their deceased ancestors dwelled there in the cliff dwellings. They were only used by their tribe in emergencies.

The Kid told the medicine man that the cliff dwellings were very beautiful and mysterious. The young braves of the village, being mischievous young boys, visited them as often as they could sneak away from the sentries posted around their village. They pretended to play war games defending their village from enemies.

The Kid and his friends could stay in the cliff dwellings all day and never get bored. It seemed like every time they went there they found something new and cool to occupy their time. They camped there overnight a couple of times hoping to meet some of their ancestors. They dreamed about living there permanently. The cliff dwellings were their special hangout place.

They had rope climbing races to see who could get to the top the fastest. The Kid was the reigning champion. Once they arrived at the first level of the dwellings, they went from room to room checking out everything. There were ladders set up inside the building that enabled them to climb to the different levels of building. The wooden built ladders seemed to be like new. They could only guess they were in great condition because they were stored in a place that was hidden from the elements. The building was four stories high that was built into the mountain. They especially loved the top level, which was the lookout tower. From the top level they could see the dust kicked up of any other raiding parties coming their way for a hundred miles, on a clear day.

There were three villages that encompassed the Pinal Apache Nation. The main village was in Aravaipa Canyon, and it was there where Chief Eskiminzin lived. He was the big chief of their Nation. The Kid's village at Wheatfield's was located about seventy miles north of the main village. Then another village was located about forty miles south of Aravaipa Canyon, called Cushing, their chief was Natches.

In April of 1871, a horrible event occurred at the village of Cushing, located about forty miles south of Camp Verde. This event would ever stain relations between the Apaches, the White's, the

Mexicans and the Papago Indians. On that day a group of men out of Tucson, many of whom were Papago Indians and Mexicans, their leaders being Americans, treacherously attacked the peaceful, sleeping the Apache village at Cushing. One hundred and forty-four Apaches were killed in the massacre. Sadly, most of the dead were women and children. The event became cause for national debate. Many citizens in the East were horrified and even President Ulysses S. Grant denounced it as a cold blooded act.

However, in Arizona very few people were sympathetic. Even though the dead were for the most part innocent children and women, they were Apache and were lumped in with all the renegades, but sadly though these folks had nothing to do with any fighting. They were farmers and raised livestock. The perpetrators were captured and brought to trial a year later. They were all acquitted. One of the principal leaders was Sidney De Long, who was later elected mayor of Tucson.

There was a young commander on duty at nearby Camp Grant at time of the incident. Camp Grant was only a couple of miles from Cushing. He was sympathetic to the Apache. His name was Lieutenant Royal E. Whitman. Because of the way he stood up for the Apache, Chief Eskiminzin considered him a close friend. Lieutenant Whitman was heartsick over the murder of innocent people.

Out on patrol that day Lieutenant Whitman and his troop were on maneuvers in the area and just happened to come upon the slaughter, right after the murdering event occurred. In his report he mentions that his troop buried the bodies of the dead and did what they could to console those that survived as well as treating the injured survivors.

In his report Whitman related that coming upon the slaughter he said, was the most inhumane site of carnage he had ever encountered, even worse than the way the Union Army troops were treated at the Confederate Prison in Andersonville, during the Civil War. He went on to write in his report, that even the many depravations during the Civil War had nothing on the wanton slaughter of innocent people that he witnessed there at Cushing.

Lieutenant Whitman and his men escorted the survivors to nearby Camp Grant after they recovered from their wounds and were able to travel. From there the survivors were taken to the main Pinal Apache village deep in Aravaipa Canyon. For his compassion Lieutenant Whitman was court-martialed several times and finally forced out of the army. General George Stoneman, the commander at Camp Grant also being sympathetic to the plight of the Apaches, was relieved of his command over the incident.

Chief Eskiminzin was very devastated over the wanton slaughter of his people at Cushing. So, he notified Toga-de-chuz, the Apache Kid's father at

"Wheatfields," they needed to pack up their belongings and move to the main village in Aravaipa Canyon. He felt that after the slaughter at Cushing, they would only be safe in the main village. The Chief said;

> *"If this could happen once it could happen again. And we need to be prepared."*

The medicine man went on to say that;

> *"Chief Eskiminzin was known to be a very wise and intelligent leader. He would fight only as a last resort. He always strived for peace."*

Chief Eskiminzin always tested the methods of peace before war because he believed nothing good came from the taking lives.

Below is a photo of Chief Eskiminzin with two of his ten children, that was found in our National Archives.

Again the main village was located deep in Arvavaipa Canyon and had only two ways into the village, following Aravaipa Creek from the west and the east traveling from along Ariavaipa Creek to where it meets up with Turkey Creek. The Galiuro Mountain range was rugged, the canyon was deep and narrow so anyone approaching the village was seen or heard for miles.

About two miles west of the main village in the canyon, the river narrowed to about twenty feet wide and that narrow stretch ran for about a half mile. It was very easy to hear or see anyone coming toward their village from that direction but coming from the west was a little more of a challenge to stand guard. Again the terrain was still very rugged but intruders could be seen following the creek.

The main village in Aravapai Canyon was easy to defend and he had plenty of braves that pulled sentry duty. Sentries were posted twenty-four hours a day at each end of the canyon a couple of miles in each direction of the village. The sentries had several ways to get messages to the other position, including using mirrors during the day to send messages, animal cries at night and smoke signals were used for long range signaling.

The Kid told the old medicine man that he remembered the day they left their home village at Wheatfields like it was yesterday. He told the medicine man that;

*"He and his friends wept as they
the left. All they could think about
was that they might never see their
beloved cliff dwellings again. It was
almost like a part of their hearts had
been ripped out of their chests."*

Called the Hidden Canyon of the Aravaipa
their new home was located about twenty-five
miles south and east of Mount Graham in the
Galiuro Mountain range. It was about ninety miles
southeast of Wheatfields. It took them four days
to travel from Wheatfield's to the main village in
Aravaipa Canyon. As they approached the
beginning of Aravaipa Canyon, Togo-de-Chuz
could see the boys were not happy about where
they were going and leaving their beloved cliff
dwellings for this God forsaken place hot dry
desert area, so they thought. He knew they would
never understand why they had to leave their
beautiful village.

Once they arrived at the mouth of Aravaipa
Canyon, he finally had the nerve to ask his father
if this God forsaken place would be their new
home. Togo-de-Chuz just laughed. He told his
son and his friends that their new home was a
paradise. The Kid said he told his father;

*"Hopefully, but from what we can
see this place is horrible. He said he
could not imagine any beauty in this
area."*

Below is a photo of rugged terrain at the mouth of Aravapai Canyon in the distance.

The Galiuro Mountain Range is a beautiful range but again they are very rugged mountains with huge deep canyons. As they started into the Canyon the terrain started to change for the better. At first they went through farmland while they followed the creek. The Kid relayed to the old medicine man that they traveled about eight more miles when ran into the confluents of Turkey Creek which ran into Aravaipa Creek. He said they followed Turkey Creek for about seven miles and then ran directly into the main village.

Below is a photo of the lush interior of Aravapai Canyon and the Aravapai Creek that was taken a few miles downstream from Chief Eskiminzin's village. One can see how the rough terrain starts to look amazing. This photo is courtesy of Arizona Hiking.com.

There were a lot of trees and plants that were on both sides of Turkey Creek. The trail crossed the creek many times along the ride. The village was located deep inside the canyon and about eight miles from the confluence of the two creeks. From start to finish Aravaipa creek runs about twenty-five miles through the Canyon. The creek is fed by several natural springs and it is comprised of wooded canyons, lush grazing areas, plentiful game, and awe-inspiring sandstone cliffs.

If the reader looks closely at the picture on the next page, one can see the lush land in the valley at the bottom of the cliffs that is where the picture above was taken. It is the middle of the canyon. The Apaches learned to adapt to the land of the Arizona deserts. Again the villagers killed only for food and they defended their land with amazing skill as they knew every nook and cranny in their land.

The location of the village was a virtual paradise. He also went on to say that Chief Eskiminzin was born and raised in Aravaipa Canyon and never left. The Chief was very excited to have his brother Toga-De-Chuz, of Captain Chiquito and their village in the safety of Aravaipa Canyon. The placement of the village was in a clearing between two streams and was surrounded by huge impassable cliffs. They had vegetable gardens and plenty of room for the livestock to graze. The area was surrounded by beautiful trees and natural plants. The Kid said it was hard to believe this peaceful paradise could exist from where they started into the canyon.

The reader can see just by looking at the picture below found in our National Archives, that the location of the village down in the canyon was a perfect natural fortress provided by the steep cliffs and mountains.

According to the Kid the first day they arrived at their new home most of the day was spent unpacking. That evening Chief Eskiminzin threw a big dinner party when they finished moving into their homes. The Chief was excited to have his whole tribe now within the safety of main village.

The Kid said the first time he saw Eskiminzin's oldest daughter, he knew it was love at first sight. He knew he wanted her to be his wife the minute they made eye contact. She was unusually tall with long black hair. He thought she was the most beautiful maiden he had ever seen. He knew that neither of them was ready to be married but when the time came he knew he wanted her hand in marriage. His obstacle would not be her but her father. He needed to impress the chief with lots of horses and most of all have several heroic deeds in his resume for the chief to give his daughter's hand in marriage. An Apache woman was very much a hot commodity in their communities. They could cook, raise children, tan hides, make clothing, hunt and raise crops. None of that mattered to him though, because all he wanted was her sleeping with him in his Wickieup.

In May of 1872 just about one year after they moved into their new village, word came that the great white father was sending his representative to meet with Chief Eskiminzin with the idea of setting a long term peace treaty. The meeting was set for May 21 and 22nd, 1872 at nearby Camp Grant. The president sent Brigadier General Oliver Otis Howard to confer with General Crook, who the Apaches called Nantan

Lupan, Nantan is the word for chief in the Apache language and Lupan is the name of the wolf. Because General Crook sported a full beard, which the Indians had never seen they called him Nantan Lupan.

Most of the important leaders of the southwest were in attendance at the meeting, including Indian leaders, Mexican leaders and leading Americans politicians from across the southwest. The success of the conference depended entirely on Chief Eskiminzin's willingness to negotiate.

Chief Eskiminzin wanted the members of the conference to ensure: (1) that his people would be given their own reservation. (2) that the peace treaty be maintained by both the white man and the Apaches. (3) J. E. Roberts to be assigned as agent for the Apaches and (4) the Apache children that had been taken captive at the Cushing raid to be returned to their families. General Howard agreed to the first three conditions, but said he was only able to find six of the 28 captive children. The general told the chief he did not know if the rest of the children would be returned as soon as possible.

Unbeknown too Chief Eskiminzin, General Howard came to Camp Grant with the idea that Chief Eskiminzin and his Pinal Apache tribe would be the first tribe to be moved to the newly to be formed San Carlos Apache Indian reservation. It was a stroke of luck that Chief Eskiminzin was thinking along the same lines as the General. He wanted his people safe and he thought they would be safe under government protection, although, he was not thrilled to have to leave his beloved village where he lived his whole life.

The next day General Howard agreed to all of the terms and told Chief Eskiminzin that the six captured children had been taken to Camp Grant and would remain there until all of the remaining children could be found. Chief Eskiminzin agreed to the terms. The General assured the Chief that the families of the children could visit them until all were found and then they would all be returned to their families at The San Carlos Reservation.

Placing a stone near the site of the conference, Chief Eskiminzin stated;

> "As long as that stone lasts, no more campaigns shall be made by my people. Every day of peace we will put another rock on the pile. This would serve as a signal to all that peace is going to be their future way of life."

Two days after the meeting, General Howard accompanied by Eskiminzin, Captain Chaquito and Togo-de-Chu, went in a search of a location for their new reservation. Within in a few days they all made the decision that the reservation would be located at the confluents of the Gila and the San Carlos Rivers and it would be called the San Carlos Apache Indian Reservation. Then they set the boundaries of the reservation which consisted of one million eight hundred thousand total acres of land and these boundaries would encompass the entire reservation. In December of 1872 the San Carlos Apache Indian Reservation was established.

According to the medicine man, General Crook had more difficulty moving the Chiricahua Apaches to the San Carlos reservation than their Pinal, White Mountain or Yavapai Tribes. Cochise finally agreed to move his tribe and to join Chief Eskiminzin and the Pinal Apaches after he made peace ending his twelve-year long war against the whites and Mexicans. The only stipulation Cochise had was that he wanted his own reservation. During their second meeting General Crook told Cochise that the Great White father agreed to eventually let him have his own reservation in the Dragoon Mountains but for now part of the agreement was that he would move his people to San Carlos to show good faith.

General Crook was very happy with Cochise decision to move, because the Chirachaua Tribe was the most respected and the fiercest of all Apaches and it would make it a lot easier for him to move the rest of the Apaches nations to the reservation once they heard that Cochise had made the decision to settle his differences, make peace and move his people to the San Carlos. General Crook told the chiefs of all the Apache Nations that once the reservation was up and running and all was well that their own reservations would be set aside by the government so they could move back to their own lands and those lands would be set aside permanently as their own reservations. Cochise told all of his braves that he trusted General Crook and they would eventually be back in their own land if they abided by the treaty.

During the meeting Cochise told all present that the white man had endless numbers and would continue to invade their land and the Apache numbers were dwindling at an alarming pace. He convinced most of the leaders of the various tribes that the only way they would survive was move to the reservation where they would be safe and could become farmers and trade their handmade dry goods for needed supplies. He explained that the reservation system worked for all the tribes in the east and there was no reason why the reservation system would not work for the Apache Nations.

Some of the young braves expressed concern because the white man had broken every treaty that had ever been set in the past. One of the more trusted elder braves, Geronimo, fiercely objected to moving to the reservation saying he wanted to live the old ways, which was to rob and steal from the whites and Mexicans. Cochise said it was the hardest decision he had to make when he expelled his lifelong friend and brother Geronimo from the meeting and informed him that if he was not willing to go to move to San Carlos that he would be considered an enemy from that day forward until he agreed to give up the old ways, raiding other tribes, the Mexicans and the whites.

We are going to touch a little on Geronimo because he is an interesting story for sure but he also had a profound effect on the life of the Apache Kid. They hated each other but they had the utmost respect for each other.

Geronimo's Apache name was Goy-Ath-lay which means *"One Who Yawns."* General Crook in his memoirs called Geronimo a *"human tiger."*

Geronimo was born near Turkey Creek in June of 1829. His grandfather, Naco, was a Mogollon Apache Indian chief and his father became a Mimbreno Apache when he married Geronimo's mother. Thus Geronimo was borne into the tribe of Mangas Coloradas, the Mimbreno Chief. Around 1864 he married an Apache woman, Alope and very soon they had three daughters.

Sometime late in the year 1868, Geronimo and the braves from his tribe went to the great trading center at Casas Grandes, Mexico. One evening they made camp near Presidio del Janos, Chihuahua, Mexico. Until that time, they were enjoying a peaceful life. The next morning Geronimo and his braves decided to go to Janos to trade goods with the Mexican merchants that lived in Janos like they had done for many years. As usual they left their women and children at their camp, while they went to do their trading.

In the nearby state of Sonora, Mexico a general by the name of Carrasco was the governor and a dictator. When he found out that there was a large number of Apaches were living in and around Janos, he immediately gathered his forces.

Although he had no authority in the state of Chihuahua he set out for Janos and ordered his forces to march on the Apache encampment while the braves were in town trading on their trading trip. His soldiers killed scores of women and children. The surviving ninety women and children captured and were sold as slaves.

When Geronimo and the rest of his braves returned from their trading venture they found the bloody carnage, it was then that he found the bodies of his wife, his mother and his three daughters who had been slaughtered in the raid. He stayed there for one full day just staring at his dead family. He was in total shock and later said he felt like he had no soul. From that day forward he hated everyone who was not Apache.

At the same meeting that Cochise signed the treaty, one of his son's, Naiche told his father he did not want to go to the reservation but assured his father that he would not cause trouble and that anyone who went with him to the Pa-Gotzin-Kay plateau in the Sierra Madre Mountains in Mexico could live in peace. He assured his father they would be farmers, raise livestock and trade goods with the Mexicans for supplies they needed.

The plateau was two miles wide and five miles long and was located high in the Sierra Madre mountain range in Mexico. The plateau was very fertile and water was abundant. It was a perfect location to raise crops and cattle and it was also a natural fortress. Three sides of the plateau are protected by the flow of the Yaqui River and the fourth side the mountains were so steep and rugged that it was impassible except for one very rough trail to the top. The Plateau was easily protected at the pass with sentries posted along the trail and was virtually impossible to approach without being seen for several miles. Naiche and his tribe would be forever known as the Nameless ones.

Every Apache that lived on the reservation was tattooed with a specific brand somewhere on their body that was visible for all to see. Generally, the distinguishing tattoo was placed in the middle of their forehead, wrist or arm. Then the army would record each brand with that Apache and a personal record was kept in an army register. If they never went to the reservation, they were never branded.

Naiche was appalled that they were treated like cattle. So he and all of his followers moved to Mexico and were forever known as the Nameless ones because the US Army had no record of them.

This brutal act in this author's estimation was an indication of governments stand with regard to the people that were the original inhabitants of the territory. Rather than try to live with these Native Americans they were treated worse than slaves.

The picture on the next page is of the Pa-Gotzin-Kay Plauteau, during the rainy season, and is in the background, was provided by hiking.com and used with their permission. The plateau has fertile land with abundant water used to raise animals and grow crops. There is only one trail leading to the top, so it is easy to defend and guard. The balance of sides of the plateau is almost impossible to ascend. It was a perfect natural hideout the Apache used for centuries. They traded their animals and crops at the nearby Mexican villages for other supplies.

Chapter Four

General George Crook started the process of moving the various tribes and their villages to the new reservation in early 1873. Chief Eskiminzin and his Pinal Apache were the first to be moved to the reservation, mainly because they were the closest village to the new San Carlos Reservation. Most of the other tribes including the Chiricahua were all having great difficulties moving to the reservation. They were suffering major power struggles within their tribes because some braves wanted to live the old way. During these power struggles Geronimo's band of renegades grew in numbers as the young braves that wanted to keep the old ways left their various villages to join his gang of renegades.

The Kid told the medicine man that he knew they would be one of the first tribes to move for two reasons, first because they were located the closest to the San Carlos Reservation and secondly Eskiminzin already prepared the village for the move. The told the medicine man that the whole village was packed and ready to go when the Army arrived at their village in Aravapai Canyon.

It was late February of 1873 when the Army arrived at Chief Eskiminizin's village in Aravapai Canyon, to escort the people to the nearby San Carlos Reservation. The first folks to arrive at their camp were the Army Scouts. They were Chief of Scouts Al Sieber, Clay Beauford, Big Tom Sisson, who would later be involved in one of the most famous Gunfights and manhunts in Arizona history, along with several Apache scouts.

Tom Sisson was a very interesting character. After he retired from the army where he worked in and around the Aravapai Valley for several ranchers and finally ended up working with the Power family in Rattlesnake Canyon which was just one canyon south of Aravapai Canyon. It too was also a very rugged canyon. Sisson was involved in the most notorious shootout in the Arizona history, while defending the family gold mine and along with Tom and John Power, was sentenced and served the longest prison sentences in Arizona History.

Al Sieber, the most experienced scout among the group at that time held the title of Sergeant of Scouts and led the troops that moved the Kid's village in Aravapai Canyon. Al along with Tom, spoke all the dialects of the different Apache languages, so there was no way the Apaches could talk around Al or Tom without them knowing what they were saying or what they were planning.

The leader of the army company was Lieutenant Britton Davis and the chief scout was Clay Beauford. Clay was a retired confederate soldier, who had moved out west after the civil war, looking for excitement. He was a jolly fellow, well over six feet tall and weighed in excess of two hundred fifty pounds but he had a quick wit and jolly personality. The medicine man said the

Kid's father and chief Eskiminzin were the first ones to meet Lieutenant Davis when they arrived at the village. The first thing the Kid noticed was that Clay Beauford rode a beautiful large roan horse that stood eighteen hands high.

All of the young braves ran right up to Clay not just to see him but because they wanted to get a closer look at his beautiful horse. Clay Beauford was very impressed at the Kid's knowledge of horseflesh. He could also see that the young man was a born leader. He kept the rest of the boys at bay and did all of the talking. After all of the wagons were loaded and they were about to start their trek to San Carlos, Clay Beauford asked the boy's father, if his son could ride along with he and the Lieutenant Davis. Beauford told Toga-de-Chuz he had an extra mount and that he saw great leadership potential in his young son and he wanted to get to know the Kid.

It was quite an honor to be invited to ride with the army chief of scouts. Clay and the Kid seemed to hit it right off the minute they met. The Kid had made a special friendship with Beauford that would end up being a lifelong friendship and who had a great influence in the Kid's early life. They started conversing as soon as Beauford brought over the army mule for the young brave to ride. The youngster told Clay he was excited to be able to ride a trained Army mule. He told Clay he had seen them in the past but never had the chance to ride one. In passing the Kid told Clay not only were the mules well trained but they were good eating and considered a delicacy to the Apache. Clay laughed and told the Kid;

> *"I would have never guessed but*
> *then again I have never been hungry*
> *enough to eat a mule, but it doesn't*
> *sound to appetizing to me."*

Then Clay just smiled and told the young boy that he could not believe he knew so much about horses and mules. Clay told the Kid he knew the Apaches loved to steal government trained mules. They were more sure footed than horses and could travel long distances with small amounts of water and food.

Al Seiber the scout in the lead of the troops that accompanied their troop was one of the greatest scouts the Arizona history. Sieber acquired his scouting skills from the Seminole Indians while fighting in the Civil War. His truly remarkable skills were admired by both the Indians and the white man alike. He was not only respected his scouting skills, but again he was able to speak their language so he was a perfect person to take to any and all meetings as a trusted interpreter. His scouting exploits are among the most thrilling ever.

Albert "Al" Sieber was born in Heidelberg Germany on February 29th 1844, a leap year, in a small village near Heidelberg Germany. His family immigrated to the United States when Al was just a child and settled in Lancaster, Pennsylvania, then the family moved to Minnesota. At the age of 18, Al enlisted in Company B of the Minnesota Infantry. During the Civil war he served valiantly at Antietam, Fredericksburg and Gettysburg, where he received permanent wounds that would plague him for his entire life. He had over eighteen scares on his body from knife and bullet wounds.

After the Civil War ended, like many young men at that time, the east held no appeal. Al decided to go west *"where the action was."* Sieber prospected for a while in both California and Nevada, but in 1866 he arrived in the newly formed town of Prescott, Arizona. He began managing a ranch there and also began learning his remarkable Indian tracking and fighting stills.

The nearby Yavapai Apache villagers taught him how to speak the Apache language, which would be one of his most valuable skills. By 1871 Al Seiber was well known throughout the territory for his scouting skills. While at Fort Whipple near the town of Prescott he became friends with General George Crook. So impressed with his scouting skills and his ability to speak the Apache language, General Crook hired him to be the sergeant of Scouts for his army troop. Al Seiber along with Lieutenant Britton Davis, Clay Beauford and Tom Sisson were all great influences in the life of the young Apache brave.

The young man also took a liking to the scout, Big Tom Sisson who was the person, was responsible for bestowing him with the name *"The Kid,"* Sisson he said that the young brave was simply too long and too hard to remember so the new name stuck with him for the rest of his life.

Sisson was a good scout but was not on the same skill level as Clay and Al. The old Indian told the author they shared a lot of good times through the years. Tom also had a great sense of humor and was not too great with a pistol but was a tremendous shot with a Springfield 303 rifle.

The old medicine man went on to say that Clay did most of the talking for the first ten miles and since the Kid was only thirteen years old at the time and he didn't have a lot to talk about but he was a good listener. The Kid told Clay all about growing up in Wheatfields and hanging out in the cliff dwellings by their village. Clay told the Kid he visited the cliff dwellings when they were out on maneuvers just a couple of months earlier. Clay told the Kid he noticed the ropes were gone and there was no way to climb up to the lower level of the buildings but he enjoyed the Kid telling him all about the building because the Kid knew every inch of the complete four story building.

For the next forty miles Clay Beauford talked about himself. He told the Kid he was a Major in the Confederate Army during the Civil War. Clay said he actually rode with General Stonewall Jackson and was with the General during the war. He said the General was mortally wounded on the morning of May the 2nd, 1863 at Chancellorsville, Virginia. The general died of his wounds eight days later. Clay told the kid, he was injured but the General took the main hit. Clay went on to say once he healed from his wounds, he became a scout and that two Seminole Indians taught him his scouting skills. He also spoke fluent Apache. They spent the whole trip talking about scouting skills. The Kid was a sponge for Clay's words. After Clay discussed different situations he would ask the Kid what he would do and what he would look for. By the time they arrived at San Carlos Clay was amazed at all the Kid remembered about what he taught him about scouting during their ride. The Kid enjoyed Clay's companionship so he hung out with Clay as often as possible.

The Kid was bored living on the reservation so after a couple of years, he obtained special permission from the Indian Agent to take a job working in nearby Globe where he employed at a local feed store, his job was to help load customer's wagons with the feed and seeds, they had purchased at the store. After that, he upgraded himself, when he obtained a job working at the stockyards feeding and watering the livestock.

The Indians on the reservation were provided beef regularly issued by the U.S. Government. They preferred to have the steers shot in an open corral and then they would skin and dress the beef carcasses themselves. The Kid owed his ability as a marksman to the fact that he was given the job by his friend John Redmond to kill the corralled animals. With his carbine he would walk around the six-inch wide catwalk atop the corral fences, and when an animal looked in his direction he fired without pausing in his stride. At each crack of his rifle a beef fell with a bullet hole in the curl of hair directly at the center of the animal's forehead.

He bought his first pair of jeans and cowboy boots with his first paycheck. He traveled back and forth from the reservation to his job in town each day. It was about a ten-mile ride from their home to Globe. The first Friday he arrived back at the reservation wearing his new boots and jeans he met Clay at the Indian Agents office. Clay smiled and told the kid he loved his new look. He invited the Kid to his sleeping barracks and gave him his first western style shirt. He told the Kid he needed to look the part of a cowboy. The Kid wore those pants and shirt until they could stand up by themselves at night when he undressed for bed. He washed his clothes once a week. It wasn't long before he had three pairs of jeans and four shirts.

The Kid told Beauford and all of the guys down at the stockyards ribbed him me about his wardrobe. He said;

> *"He didn't care if they called him names. He said he was loving life."*

He simply did what Clay Beauford taught him and just laughed a lot. He said he prided himself on being trustworthy and friendly. He even told them he would be a chief someday. The kid became popular around Globe.

The Chiricahua Apache tribe was the next tribe to be moved to San Carlos in early 1875. Sadly, Cochise passed away on June 2nd 1874 and would never see his dream of his own reservation come to pass. His oldest son Tahzay, was the new chief and had the same temperament and logic as his father. It is said he even looked just like his father. They were guided from their home in the Dragoon Mountains to the San Carlos Indian Reservation by U.S. Army troop under the command of Lieutenant Britton Davis and one company of soldiers from Fort Bowie. It was their job to make sure they arrived without incidents. This was part of the agreement between Cochise and General Crook.

Tahzay knew there was a chance Geronimo and his band of renegade followers might cause trouble for them on the trip to San Carlos and he wanted to avoid a skirmish with Geronimo. He knew that at some point down the road his braves would end up fighting his father's boyhood friend, Geronimo and his band of renegades. He just wanted to put it off for as long as possible. For this reason, the chief asked General Crook to provide an army escort for their move to San Carlos. He agreed to back the army if they encountered the renegades on the trip.

The move went very smooth. They really did not have any problems during the six-day trip to San Carlos from Cochise Stronghold in the Dragoon Mountains. When Lieutenant Davis first laid his eyes on the San Carlos Reservation he called the place, *"Hells Forty Acres."*

In his memoirs Lieutenant Britton Davis described The San Carlos Reservations site as;

"A gravely flat confluence of the Gila and the San Carlos rivers."

The land rose thirty feet above the river bottoms and was dotted here and there by the drab adobe buildings of the Indian Agency and wickieups. Scrawny, lines of scattered cottonwood trees, shrunken, almost leafless, marked the course of the streams. Rain was so infrequent that it took on the resemblance of a phenomenon when it occurred. The place was almost continuously dry, hot, dusty and grave-laden winds swept across the plains with summer temperatures of 116 degrees in the shade was not out of the ordinary. On their first night upon their arrival at San Carlos, Lieutenant Davis had to sleep on the ground without a tent. When he woke in the morning he began to roll up his bedroll and discovered a ten-inch centipede in his bedroll that had slept with him.

Below is a photo of Al Sieber taken circa 1860. This photo was found in our National Archives.

Chapter Five

According to the Kid, two major events occurred in 1875 that would have a huge effect on his life. First, Clay Beauford, took the job as the head of the Apache Reservation Police and second, Al Sieber became Chief of Scouts. According to the Kid, one afternoon Clay Beauford came to Globe to visit him while he was working at the stockyards. Clay Beauford made no moves without a purpose and the Kid new he had something on his mind.

Clay started the conversation with the Kid by telling him that with the arrival of the Chiracahua Apache tribe at the reservation that San Carlos now was populated with over one thousand people. He told the Kid, Tom Sisson and Al Sieber, along with two Army battalions had been ordered to transfer the Yavapai Apache Nation from Camp Verde to the San Carlos Reservation. Clay told the Kid they would be bringing in an additional 1200 braves, women and children to the San Carlos Reservation. Beauford said since the population of the reservation would double and that he would have to expand his reservation police department to keep up with the new expanded population on the reservation. Clay told the Kid that he moved several of his trusted Apache Scouts over to become additional reservation police to prepare for the issues of policing the new larger population and that the reservation would be busting at the seams by the time the Yavapai arrived.

Clay went on to tell the Kid he needed to hire additional scouts to take the place of the men he transferred to the reservation police. He went on to say that he and Al Sieber had decided to offer him a job as a scout. The kid said he was thrilled to say the least. Clay told the kid they both thought he would be a great scout even if he was only fifteen years old. Clay laughed and said,

"Son I know you and you are a natural for this job."

The Kid quit his job at the general store and stockyards right on the spot and rode back to the reservation with Clay Beauford. They discussed his responsibilities as a scout, his duties and of course his pay. Beauford told the Kid he would be eligible for all of the government benefits that go with the job including retirement with pay after twenty years of service. The Kid was very excited about the opportunity to be working with his good friend and could see that with his new position he would soon be able to ask Chief Eskiminzin for the hand of his daughter, Liawana's hand in marriage. She was the love of his life and he was very excited about being in a position to settle down with her and be able support a family.

The second big event was the hiring of the new Indian Agent who would be in charge of San Carlos. The rumor was that the new agent was a man who a great vision for the people. The new agent was aware of the fact that the previous Indian agents were skimming money and supplies meant for the Apaches. He knew they were not getting their full allotment of supplies the government was sending them to the reservation in good faith. He was also sold on getting rid of the Army and planned to have the Indian Police continue to take charge of policing the reservation. He definitely sounded like a man of vision but the Kid said he was he was going to wait until he arrived to make his own assessment.

John P. Clum was the new Indian Agent at the San Carlos Apache Indian Reservation. Clum was born and raised on a farm in New Claverack near the Hudson River in the Catskill Mountains in upper New York State. He entered Rutgers University in hopes of becoming a Dutch Reformed Church Minister. Sadly, Clum never was able to obtain his dream of being a minister but he did graduate from Rutgers University, Magna Cum Laude with a Bachelor of Arts with a teaching major. He was a deeply religious man and excelled in athletics while attending Rutgers. He was on the school boxing and also played football. He was a muscular young man and already balding by his freshman year, and he was an intimidating looking presence for such a young man.

After graduating from college John decided to go west. He found a solution in a newspaper notice that the War Department was organizing a new meteorological service throughout the country. They were seeking recruits to monitor the weather. He appealed to the congressman in his district, and Clum soon received his probationary appointment observer Sergeant attached to the Army Signal Corps. He passed the required written examination, trained briefly at Fort Myer in Washington, DC and was ordered to report to the small town of Santa Fe, New Mexico, which was the capital of the territory of New Mexico.

Clum left Washington in October of 1871 for the long train and stage journey to his new post in New Mexico which was a strange land to him. Dressed as any proper young Eastern gentleman, he became increasingly self-conscious of his Derby hat, stiff shirt, jacket and trousers as he traveled further and further toward the southwest frontier. The minute he arrived at Santa Fe he went right to a mercantile store and bought a wardrobe of western wear. He decided to grow a full beard thinking he would look more mature to the Mexicans, soldiers and teamsters who made up most of the population of Santa Fe. He was only 21 years old and felt he needed to look older being around such a tough looking crowd.

His principal duties were to record atmospheric conditions six times a day and then to telegraph the results to the Chief Signal Officer in Washington, where they became part of a file of weather reports from his and the other 49 observation stations throughout the country. This daily review was the first report of the newly formed United States Weather Bureau. With obvious time to spare, John Clum established a school nearby and taught the local children mathematics, reading and writing. The local residents took their children's schooling seriously and in no time the school grew to the point that he needed to hire an assistant.

A little more than four hundred miles south of the town of Santa Fe, New Mexico, life at the San Carlos Indian Reservation was not going as well as expected. The army was still keeping the peace. The Apaches had indicated their opinion of the White Man's Rules by murdering two previous Indian agents and two Army Lieutenants and tried to kill he latest civilian administrator, James E. Roberts, who promptly resigned under pressure of death and left the Territory for unknown places. When submitting his resignation to his superiors in Washington he was quoted as saying;

> *"Any anyone who comes to the San Carlos Apache Reservation to run the place would be like walking into a hornet's nest covered with honey."*

Officials of the Bureau of Indian Affairs figured they needed a new face at the reservation, and hopefully not another scalp. So, in November of 1873, a reasonably happy twenty-year old weather observer, resolutely practicing his Spanish, teaching English, and taking climate temperatures, received a letter from the Indian Bureau inquiring as to his interest in an appointment as the Indian Agent at the San Carlos Reservation.

The Army Weather Observer and Army Sergeant, John Clum had heard much about the depredations of the Apaches in the adjoining Territory, and perhaps the very extent of the trouble represented a compelling challenge to him being a man of principle and with a strong religious background. Within a few days Clum wrote his superiors in Washington, accepting the position. He received an appointment as The Indian Agent at the San Carlos Reservation in Arizona at the age of 23 on February 27th 1874.

The reason Clum was chosen was for this offer to the young John Clum might be difficult to fathom, unless one understood the ways of the Washington Politicians. When General Grant took was elected as President, it was his policy to assign supervision of the welfare of the various Indian tribes on reservations to religious sects, with agents selected from among the respective religious denominations. It therefore seemed logical to some bureaucrats in Washington to assign one of the peace-loving members of Dutch Reformed Church. Since many Dutch Reformed students were enrolled at Rutgers, it was here the Indian Bureau official sought a recruit.

Before Clum took the job he made a visit to Rutgers, he spoke with several students telling them about his life in the west. Since he already lived in New Mexico and was already trained. The government decided he was the perfect choice. Unmentioned by the students was the fact that none of them had any desire whatsoever to volunteer for this very dangerous and unrewarding position in such a hostile place. In any case, Clum was nominated and accepted the job.

After he was nominated while in Washington for training, John Clum was inundated with forms and documents by the Bureau of Indian Affairs while he was training for his new position. While there he met Arizona's Territorial Delegate to Congress, R.C. McCormick. The first thing the Congressman said to Clum about becoming the next Indian Agent at San Carlos was;

> "Are you out of your mind? Do you know what has been happening out there to the previous Indian agents on that reservation?"

Clum fired right back at the Congressman and told him that if the previous Indian Agents had been treating the Apache's right, nothing would have happened to them.

During his lengthy stay in Washington, Clum occupied himself in a way that neither would be endorsed by the politically oriented Indian Bureau nor condoned by the War Department or the officers of its Department in Arizona. He collected reports, data, memos, and letters pertaining to the treatment of the Apaches from the treaties and to the signing of The Gadsen Purchase.

John Clum packed up all of the papers and left to go St. Louis to serve as the New Mexico Delegate of the General Assembly Convention of the Presbyterian Church. Once he was finished in St. Louis he headed for San Carlos Reservation to assume responsibilities as the new Indian Agent. He boarded a train in Chicago and went from there to San Francisco, then he caught a steamer to San Diego, then he rode a train from San Diego to Tucson and from there he rode a stage the one hundred twenty-five miles north to his destination, which was the San Carlos Reservation. The long trip provided him plenty of time to read the reports and by the time he reached San Carlos, his conclusion that was to make him decidedly irritant to the army and his superiors. Briefly the Apaches had been getting the short end of the stick and the Bureau of Indian Affairs was well aware of the decidedly sordid situation.

John Clum gradually developed sympathy for a people, who were being told their land must be handed over to the white man. He had discovered ample proof that the Apache's promises were more to be trusted than the government's. He was appalled by the obvious evidence that the Army's goal was to steal their land and to exterminate these Native Americans.

Clum arrived at the San Carlos Reservation on August 8, 1874, and after the long trip, grueling, dusty trip all the while he studied all of paperwork he had gathered he was ready to act the minute he stepped off the stagecoach. The Kid said he was with Al Sieber, Clay Beauford and Lieutenant Britton Davis were on hand when Clum arrived on the stage. According to the Kid, Clum was a sight for sore eyes, when he climbed out of the stage. The Kid said that;

"He was wearing a coon skin cap was dressed with a pair of jeans, a nice dress shirt and was wearing a leather vest. He went on to say they all looked at each other and thought, how in the hell could this guy be comfortable, wearing those hot clothes. It was August and one of the hottest summer months at the reservation. Then the Kid said he looked into Clum's eyes and all he could see was fire in them, there was no doubt he was a man on a mission."

The first question Clum asked Lieutenant Davis was;

"Point me to my office and then to my sleeping quarters." Then his second statement was, *"Is it always this damn hot, humid and miserable?"*

Lieutenant Britton Davis pointed to the building directly in front of where they were standing and then he told Clum he had arrived at the hottest most humid time of the day in the hottest month of the year. Clum answered;

"Well then it will get better?"

then, he asked the soldiers to grab his bags and follow him into his office. Clum told them that he wanted to talk to them all immediately. The Kid said it was obvious what he wanted to discuss was very important since Clum hastened them all to follow him immediately.

The picture below of John Clum was found in our National Archives. Clum is in the middle along with several Apache police and scouts.

The Kid went on to say that Clum sat behind the desk and invited everyone to sit in the chairs that were placed in front of the desk. He invited two other Apache police to come in sit and join them. He removed his hat and put it on the desk. The Kid said he was bald from above his forehead running back to the back of his head with hair only growing on the sides and that hair was short.

Clum started the meeting by telling them he had gathered a ton of memos and paperwork while in Washington for training and that while studying all of the paperwork that the government and the people they sent previously to San Carlos were out to sabotage the reservation system from the very beginning and he was appalled by the dastardly direction the government had undertaken.

Clum told everyone present at that first meeting that he was determined to see that the Apaches were going to get a square deal from that day forward. He told Lieutenant Davis that he wanted the Army off the reservation as soon as possible and it would be their responsibility to help the Apaches take complete charge of the policing and running their own reservation. He said the elections would be held in two weeks and that the reservation would be run like a democracy.

He went on to say he would only be there at San Carlos to help them make decisions. He told them he was going to open a reservation school and that his main duty would be to teach the reservation children to read and write. He told them that being educated would be the only way the Apaches could fit into and excel in the white mans society. He also asked the Kid to teach him the Apache Language and in return he would teach him how to read and write the English language. At the end of the meeting Clum asked the Indians if they had any questions or suggestions.

The Kid told his father and Captain Chiquito about the New Indian Agent Clum and his vision for their people. They were all blown away. Then he told them Clum stood up after the meeting, took off his vest and the next words out of his mouth were;

"Is it always this hot in this God forsaken place?"

The Kid said he remembered everybody there laughed. Then the Kid told Clum his new nickname would be Nantan- ben-tunny-kah-yeh. Clum asked the Kid what his nickname meant and the Kid told him that Nantan meant Chief and Ben-tunny-kah-yeh was their word for being bald or having a high forehead. Clum just laughed but he liked the name.

John Clum asked them next if there was any dinner left and then after eating dinner where were his sleeping quarters. The Kid took Clum around the grounds and introduced him to all of the chiefs including his father, his mother and Chief Eskiminzun. When they were finished with the tour the Kid's father invited Clum to join them for dinner.

During dinner Clum told went over his plan and he also insisted that they needed to elect their own leaders right away. Word spread quickly through the reservation. The people felt they truly had their first real Indian Agent. As the Kid walked with Clum around the reservation, Clum instantly received great respect from the people, they had never seen a man so young that was already balding. This was a sign of great maturity and knowledge to the Indians. His name was perfect, Nantan be-tunny-kah-yen. There was great anticipation among the people about their future and it was unanimous that they were on the road to running their own reservation and that in time the soldiers would be gone from San Carlos.

Chapter Six

The next morning according to the Kid everyone gathered in front of Clum's office to discuss the schedule for moving the Yavapai and Tonto Nations to their new home at San Carlos. This would be a huge event and would take a lot of planning to move 1200 people 180 miles of rough terrain between Fort Verde and San Carlos. Clum started by saying that the move would take place in February of 1875. General George Crook was already at Fort Verde and getting the Yavapai Apache Nation gathered at Fort Verde ready to move by December of 1874.

General Crook informed Clum that the Tonto Nation would also be present at Fort Verde sometime in December and that once he received supplies they would be ready to move that coming February of 1875. The Indian agent John Clum told them that General Crook had ordered a large supply of food, blankets and dry goods that were going to be delivered to Flagstaff by train. Then he would be transporting the goods to Fort Verde so they could be used to transport the two Apache nations to the San Carlos Reservation. Clum went on to say;

> *"It would be the Indian Scouts job to help General Crook and his troops by providing security for the trip and to make sure there were no problems with the renegade Apaches riding with Geronimo and any other group, who might try to make trouble for them on the trip."*

Agent Clum told all present he wanted the reservation elections to be held within the month so the Apaches at San Carlos had their leadership people in place before the scouts left for Camp Verde to help with the transportation of the two nations. He said it was imperative that those leaders be in place before the battalion left for Fort Verde. He went on to say that with all of his top aids gone he would not be able to run the reservation without the help of those Apache leaders and the Apache Reservation Police.

John Clum said the reservation was its own sovereign nation and that they were to enact their own laws police and rules. He wanted them to elect their own Apache leaders that would represent their people and speak for them at monthly meetings and at some point in Washington to express their dreams for their future and any issues that needed to be addressed. He said he wanted to show the politicians in Washington that they did not need the Army involved in any reservation dealings. The different chiefs, holy men and the medicine men on the reservation loved the new Agent John Clum. They knew he was the first Indian Agent that had come to the San Carlos Reservation that was fair, honest and had a dream for their future.

The months flew by. The elections went well and the leaders were in place. Clum met with the Apache leaders the day after the elections to get their input and get their layout for their plan of their future government and to give guidance. He said once the Tonto and Yavapai Nations arrived they would elect their leaders and then within a couple of months he wanted one leader elected by all of the Apache Nations at San Carlos. He said this person would be the true leader of the San Carlos Apache Reservation and he would be the main contact that would represent their people and travel to Washington with him to address any issues, with the U.S. Government officials.

Clay Beauford created the special Indian police force and trained them to keep the peace on their reservation. He also created an informer position and it was their job to keep him and Lieutenant Davis, who was in charge of the troops on the reservation informed of any problems or issues that might be brewing. It was very important that their cover not be blown for their own safety. The kid's father Toga-de-C|huz was named by Beauford to be one of those few special scout informers so and again if he or any of the other informers heard of any uprising that was being planned they could let him or Lieutenant Davis know of the plans. It was a very dangerous job but they were a very important element necessary to keep order on the reservation.

The next day the kid, along with the rest of the scouts and Lieutenant Britton Davis all met in front of Clum's office to go over the plan to move the Yavapai and Tonto Apache tribes to San Carlos. Agent Clum had a map out and started by telling them he had confirmed the trail they would use with Al Sieber Clay Beauford and Lieutenant

Britton Davis.

Clum told everyone they would be leaving for Fort Verde sometime in the middle of January. Then he went on to outline the trail for the move and said they would be taking the trail that is east of Globe that headed north through Weatfields, continuing on past the Salt River and then following Cherry Creek north to Sycamore Creek then west following the creek through the Matazal Mountains to the Verde River. He went on to say;

"This way you will be familiar with the trail to Fort Verde and this will help considerably when you bring the Tonto and Yavapai nations come back on the same trail. He said this would provide everyone complete knowledge of the area and familiarize themselves with any possible danger spots that might be lurking along the trail and the trail would allow the Indians the ability to have running water to drink, to keep their animals healthy and would allow them the ability to bathe to keep clean."

Everything involved in the move was in place by the middle of January of 1875. The Tonto Nation was at Fort Verde along with the Yavapai Nation. The supplies arrived the second week of January so the transfer began on schedule the second week of February of 1875 from Fort Verde, about one hundred and eighty miles from the San Carlos Reservation located just east of

Globe, Arizona. General Crook joined the troops for the transfer.

The renegades followed along the Verde River to the south until it met with Fossil Creek. Then from Fossil creek they met up with the East Verde River and followed it until they reached Cherry Creek then they followed Cherry Creek south past the Salt River and then onto Globe. The transfer would be an extremely dangerous operation. It was mostly due to the Al Sieber and the Apache Kid, that the operation was a success.

The transfer of the Yavapai and Tonto Apache nations that February was one of the most tragic events in Arizona history. It was one of the coldest months ever recorded with record snowfall. It involved the elderly, women and children of a most unfortunate people. About twenty-five children were born during the trip to San Carlos. A real tragedy occurred near the Matazal Mountains, which resulted in the deaths of several Indians.

They had walked a long way and several of the elderly just could not go any further. Tempers started to flare and some of the young braves broke free and started to leave the group. It was due to the bravery of both the Apache Kid and Al Sieber that a horrendous massacre was prevented. Indian Agent John Clum received word of the incident and was so concerned for the welfare of the Indians and the soldiers that he rode out to meet them at nearby *"Wheatfields,"* to help guide them himself from there to the reservation. In Britton Davis's memoirs he said;

> "*John Clum really understood the full nature of pain they endured during the trip when he saw an elderly brave who had carried his invalid wife on his back from Fort Verde to San Carlos.*"

Clum was so inspired when he saw Clum get off his horse and put the old Indian's wife on his horse and he walked with the older Indian from there to San Carlos, some forty miles. Lieutenant Davis told Agent Clum that the real hero on the trip was the Apache Kid. Davis went on to tell John Clum that without the Kids bravery and ability to reason with the Yavapai's there would have been a terrible tragedy. The Apache Kid was now considered one of most trusted Indian Scouts at the San Carlos Reservation.

The photo above taken at the San Carlos Reservation was found in our National Archives. John Clum's office is the one on the left and the building on the right was the commissary, where supplies were stored and where they were distributed to the Indians.

Below is a copy of a picture that was painted by Frederic Remington, who actually visited the San Carlos Apache Reservation, and was so moved at the site of the people lining up to get their daily rations of meat, vegetables and medicine, that he sat down in front of the commissary and painted this picture. This photo of the actual picture painted by the artist was also found in our National Archives.

Chapter Eight

Life improved remarkably almost overnight at the San Carlos Indian Reservation soon after the arrival of the John Clum. According to Britton Davis's diary, the population of the San Carlos Reservation was then well over three thousand, on a piece of land designed to hold a thousand Apache, and forcing the Indian Police Force to grow with the population to a hundred officers.

John Clum had the Indians build an earthen dam where the San Carlos River and the Gila rivers met. Then they build irrigation ditches to carry the water from the lake to their farm fields to irrigate their land. Crops grew and were harvested and farm animals were raised. The Indians were making money from the fruits of their own labor. As word spread additional nomadic Apaches began drifting into the reservation.

The photo below of construction of the canals by the Apache was found in our National Archives.

According to the Kid everything went along well at the San Carlos reservation until 1877. The only trouble that was stirring was caused by Geronimo, the leader of the last of the wild free roaming Apaches renegades, who were raiding into Southern Arizona and New Mexico from their hideout in the Sierra Madre Mountains in Mexico.

The news of Geronimo's whereabouts went through channels to General Augustus V. Kautz, the area commander of the War Department in Arizona, who passed it along to the Department of the Interior, where it was referred to the Commissioner of Indian Affairs, and somehow it ended on the desk of Indian Agent John Clum at the San Carlos Indian Reservation. Clum was given an order to capture Geronimo and bring him and his renegade followers to justice. The US Army had eleven troops of cavalry out searching for Geronimo but to no avail. The wire from the Commissioner of Indian Affairs arrived on March 20th of 1877 with a request that stated;

> *"Please take your Indian police and scouts and arrest the renegade Geronimo and his band of followers."*

Word came to Clum that Geronimo was sighted near Ojo Caliente New Mexico, which was a small trading outpost near Silver City New Mexico. Clay Beauford, the Apache Kid and about forty other reservation police and scouts were out bringing in a small village near Silver City and were halfway back to San Carlos when they were notified that Geronimo was in the area. Clay split up his troops with half continuing the transfer of the tribe to San Carlos and the other half went back to Silver City to rendezvous with John Clum and his men who were on their way by train from San Carlos, then together with Beauford's troop Clum planned to hunt down and capture Geronimo and his men.

Also not being foolish, Clum put his hostility for the military aside and asked General Crook to send troops to the Ojo Caliente area to assist in case they ran into trouble. Arrangements completed and a plan formulated, Clum and forty Indian Police from San Carlos set off on the 200-mile trip. Once at Silver City, Clum was able to requisition an additional 22 horses. Clum led the mounted troops as an advance force while Clay Beauford followed with the remaining policemen on foot.

John Clum and his men, led by scouts the Apache Kid, Messai, Chato and Rowdy, who would later win the Congressional Medal of Honor for his participation in the Apache Indian wars, arrived at Ojo Caliente on April 20th of 1877. Clum received two reports. To clear up the reports, Clum sent scouts, the Apache Kid and Chato, ahead to uncover their exact location. When they returned, the Kid reported that Geronimo was in fact camped nearby at the site of an old mining camp that had abandoned buildings for shelter and was near plenty of running water. The second report was a telegram from Fort Whipple indicating that the three cavalry troops scheduled to meet him had been delayed for two days. The

Apache Kid indicated it looked like Geronimo was getting ready to break camp and move. He told Agent Clum that for sure Geronimo and his band of renegades would definitely be gone in two days and that it would be too late if they waited for the additional troops.

According to Britton Davis's memoirs Clum was determined to go proceed with his plan to capture Geronimo and confront him before he broke camp because he was afraid the renegade would surely again slip away into nearby Mexico and freedom. He was also sympathetic with the feelings of his Apache Police and his Indian Scouts, who resented participation of the white soldiers in the plan. They thought that only Apaches have the right to catch other Apaches.

Geronimo would be aware of the presence of the mounted policemen. Clum and Davis decided to let their opponent think this constituted their entire force. He sent the Kid back to Beauford and ordered him to lead his eighty policemen quietly into the area and to hide in an empty building then not to appear until Agent Clum signaled to them by taking his hat off and scratching his head, that would be the signal for them to come out hiding and surround the renegades.

The next morning, Clum, the Kid and the rest of the scouts met with Geronimo and his band. Clum ordered the renegades back to San Carlos. Being over confident in his superior force, Geronimo refused and threatened death to all who opposed him. Clum nonchalantly removed his had and scratched his head, which was the signal for Lt. Beauford to take action. The troops hidden in the nearby building ran out and surrounded Geronimo and his followers. At that precise time, the other Indian policemen got the drop on the renegades. For the first time and the only time in his life Geronimo was captured. He and his band of renegades were put in leg irons and loaded into wagons for the ignominious trip to back to the San Carlos Indian Reservation.

Four times in the future, Geronimo would lead disgruntled renegade Indians off the reservation and go on the warpath. And four times he would surrender on his own terms usually when he got cold, hungry or tired of fighting, but he always surrendered on his own terms.

Only Agent John Clum along with The Apache Kid and Clay Beauford ever captured the wily Geronimo. Clum proposed to hang Geronimo for his murders. Had this advice been followed 500 lives and $12 million dollars would have been saved, for this was the toll of Geronimo's raids during the Apache Wars between 1882 and 1886. Sadly, for all, Indian Agent John Clum was to leave San Carlos before he could accomplish the task of following up by hanging Geronimo. Geronimo was soon released after the departure of Agent Clum.

Incredibly, after his final surrender in 1886 he was banished to Florida and became a folk hero, he was allowed to sell photos and autographs outside the reservation where he was kept as a prisoner of war. He appeared at the World Expositions in Omaha, Buffalo and St Louis. Climaxing his life as a hero, Geronimo rode behind the Army Band in the 1905 inauguration of President Theodore Roosevelt and acknowledged the cheer of the crowds. He was treated like a celebrity. He actually had over ten thousand dollars in his personal bank account when he passed away in 1913. He had learned how to live and prosper in the white mans world. This would be his final laugh at the Whites.

Geronimo along with Yahnoza far left then chappo next to him and Fun standing next to Geronimo this picture was taken the last time he surrendered to General Nelson Miles in 1885. This photo was found in our National Archives.

John Clum left San Carlos in 1877. He was offered a job in Tucson for a government civil engineering contractor in the private sector, effectively doubling his salary. He was to be married and knew he could not take his fiancée to live at the San Carlos reservation so he took a job in Tucson. His Fiancée Mary Dennison Ware met him in Tucson a week after he arrived and they were married. They lived there until 1880 when they moved to Tombstone where John founded the Tombstone Epitaph, became the mayor of Tombstone and a lifelong friend of Wyatt Earp.

On an interesting note, two years prior to before John Clum's death, he returned an Alumni questionnaire to the Rutgers University. One of the questions he had to answer was to share his life accomplishments. John Clum had been involved in many great accomplishments, but he only listed two. One was being appointed the Indian Agent at the San Carlos Apache Reservation and organizing the Indians to run their own reservation. His second noted accomplishment was to start the first Post Office in Nome, Alaska, ironically, there was no mention of being editor of the Tombstone Epitaph or anything about the gunfight at the Ok corral or being Wyatt Earp's lifelong friend.

The picture on the previous page was also found in our National Archives of John Clum and Wyatt Earp, was taken in Nome, Alaska circa 1900. Wyatt Earp is in the Middle, John Clum is to his right and their mutual friend Ed Englestadt is pictured on the left.

Below in this picture are the me who served as pallbearers at Wyatt Earp's funeral, that was found in our National Archives, and was taken in 1929 All of these men were Earp's lifelong friends. From left to right: W.J. Hunsaker, George Parsons, John Clum, Silent Film Western Actor, William S. Hart, Wilson Mizner, and the famous Film Western Actor of all time Tom Mix. John Clum passed away of natural causes on May 2, 1932 just three years after his lifelong friend Wyatt Earp passed.

Chapter Nine

Lieutenant Britton Davis was in charge of the reservation police and scouts while the government looked to appoint a new Indian Agent to replace John Clum. It was a year later before the new Indian Agent, Captain Francis E. Pierce reported to the San Carlos Reservation. He was a good also religious man and wanted the reservation to run the same way his predecessor John Clum started.

By the summer of 1880 though, conditions were truly unbearable on the San Carlos Reservation. The reservation had suffered through a drought for the previous two years. The lake that lied behind the earthen dam was dry. The Indians could not get plants to grow because of the drought. The crops and animals were also dying of thirst.

Captain Pierce kept requisitioned equipment to dig wells and tried to get his budget increased so he could requisition more food, clothing and medical help and supplies. It seemed like his requisitions were falling on deaf ears.

The Apaches were starving, poorly clothed, suffering from diseases Smallpox, Malaria and Tuberculosis. Most of all they longed for their mountain homeland. The population of the reservation had grown to 3500 on a reservation that was designed to house 1000 inhabitants. Forced to farm, they were angry and resentful. They were a very proud people and did not like relying on handouts from the US Government.

The Apache wanted to take care of themselves on their terms. Some of them had to walk twenty miles to the commissary to get their daily rations. If the old people or children were absent or unable to travel, they would not receive their rations. The local ranchers perceived the reservation as nothing other than feeding stations for the Indians, who once fed would then go out and raid again.

Under such conditions and hostility, with the Apaches fearing for their own existence, it was no surprise there were frequent breakouts from the San Carlos Reservation. The first to leave was the chief of the Warm Springs Apaches, Victorio, along with a remarkably old chief Nana. Victorio, like many other Apache Warrior Chiefs, was convinced that the US government wanted to wipe out the Apaches. Their band of renegades grew to two hundred Mescalero and Chiracahua Apaches.

They raided in Old Mexico and in southern New Mexico and Arizona. The US Government placed a bounty of $3000 on Victorio's head, and in October of 1880 Victorio and the 78 braves that were left in his band trapped and slaughtered by Mexican troops near Tres Castillos, which was just south of the border in west Texas.

Old Chief Nana amazingly escaped with 40 braves and went to the Pa-Gotzin-Kay plateau in Old Mexico to hide and escape from the US Army and eluded US and Mexican troops for two years, eventually returning to Arizona in early 1881, where he joined ranks with Geronimo.

In late June of 1881 with Geronimo back on the reservation for the third time and living at Cibecure Creek, of course only because his braves were tired and hungry, a religious leader by the name of Noch-ay-del-kline at Cibecue Creek on the San Carlos Reservation began preaching that two dead beloved Apache Leaders would be resurrected and the white man would leave Apache Country. The military began to fear his influence. So on August 28th of 1881 US Army sent Colonel Eugene Carr in charge of the 6th cavalry to Cibecue Creek to put a halt to what they thought or feared was a major uprising in the making.

Those involved in this incredible event were D Troop under the command of Lieutenant Hentig; E Troop under the command of Lieutenant Stanton; 1st Sergent Apache Mose (called Cut Mouth); Apache Sergeant Dutchy Dead Shot; Army Scout Apache Dandy Jim; Army Scout Apache Skit Shea (known as Skippy); Along with 12 scouts under the command of Apache Scout Pedro and 13 other Apache scouts in the Cibecue band.

As army Apache scout Sanchez tried to warn Noch-ay-del-kline they were there to arrest him, the army attacked the renegades and the medicine man was shot and killed. Sanchez reported he was caught in the middle. He really did not want to be involved in the fight, but realizing the only way out at that same time was to shoot his way out, he fought his way through D Troop and made his escape. However, others were not so lucky.

The firefight became chaotic and very random with shooting and killing coming from all sides. Each band of Apache Scouts fired on the other band with the army being caught in the middle. Among those who perished in the firefight were Lieutenant Hentig who was shot by either Dutchey Dead Shot or Dandy Jim, along with many Apache Renegades and Apache Scouts from each band.

It took many months of investigation for the army to figure out what went wrong at Cibecue Creek, who was responsible for the carnage and last but not least who killed Lieutenant Hentig. Those arrested after a lengthly investigation were Dutchey Dead Shot, who was proven to have shot Lieutenant Hentig at close range with a pistol and probably got his name from the fact that he was a marksman and was very popular with both whites and the Apaches. Dutchey Dead Shot was a Sergeant in the US Army. Also arrested for treason and insubordination were Apache Army Scouts Dandy Jim and Skit Shea.

All three along with five other scouts who were, UcLenny, Moese (Cut Mouth), Moseby, Battolosh and Tsoe were all taken to Fort Lowell to be court martialed by the army. When the trial ended, Dutchey Dead Shot, Dandy Jim, Skit Shea and two of the other Apache scouts were found guilty and sentenced to death by hanging. The sentence was carried out on March 3rd of 1882.

The photo below of the suspected Apache prisoners from the Cibicue firefight was found in our National Archives. Scouts Dandy Jim is on the left and Skit Shea on the right. Both are pictured with their leg irons on and being held by three-armed Apache Scouts. This picture was taken just after they arrived at Fort Lowell.

Geronimo and a White Mountain Apache Chief by the name of Natiotish took part in the melee and they both decided to flee the reservation in opposite directions for fear of severe punishment. After the skirmish they along with several young braves jumped the reservation and went on the warpath.

Geronimo fled south to Mexico and Natiotish with several of his loyal warriors ambushed and killed four San Carlos Policemen, including the police chief, "Cibecue Charley" Colvin, then Natiotish took seventy disheartened braves and headed north from of San Carlos traveling north through Wheatfields and then they folowed Cherry Creek into the Tonto Basin. They raided several ranches for supplies and left more than ten people dead in their wake.

Natiotish and his braves avoided the town of Payson going a little east following the East Verde River and camped in and around what is now a community called Whispering Pines. As they rode north and east following the river they came upon the Meadows family ranch which was located about ten miles north and east of present day Payson, Arizona. They stopped at the natural spring and salt mine that was located on the Meadows family ranch. They were in dire need of water and supplies. The Meadows being caring and hospitable let them do their thing.

Repayment for being hospitable was an out and out attack on the Meadows family ranch, which left the family patriarch and founder John Meadows and one of his son's dead after the firefight. The oldest son, Abram Meadows aka *"Arizona Charlie,"* just happened to be away, in Payson organizing the first Arizona Rodeo. When he returned a day after the attack he found his dead brother and father. Luckily, the Meadows family members were a very resourceful group, great fighters and were able to hold off the terrorizing Apaches from their well fortified home.

Abram Meadows, the oldest Meadows son and the best marksman in the family never forgave himself for not being home with his family when the attack occurred. He was an amazing rodeo cowboy and all around shooter and knew if he had been there he would have made a difference. Later changing his name to Arizona Charlie and went on to be one of the most famous rodeo cowboy's in the Arizona Territory history. Later in his career he toured the world with the Buffalo Bill Wild West Show and once played poker with Doc Holliday and Tom Horn while they were in Prescott.

The picture below taken by the author is from the rear of the Meadows property nearby cabin of friends Rich and Margie Squire, whose cabin about less than a quarter of a mile from the old Meadows Ranch. The spring runs out of the ground and into the East Verde River. It comes out of the ground, ten inches in diameter, at 68 degrees, 365 days a year. In the picture below the reader can see the spring running into the creek.

Then after raiding the Meadows ranch, Natiotish and his braves continued past the East Verde River and up a trail that led to the top of the Mogollon Rim intending to camp at General Springs, a well known watering hole on the General Crook Trail, just north and west of Payson, right near where East Clear Creek cuts a precipitous gorge into the Mogollon Rim which leads to Fort Verde.

Natiotish planned to ambush Captain Chaffee at a canyon near General Springs on the Mogollon Rim on July 17, 1882. The chief could see Captain Adna Chaffee's Company of the 6th Cavalry troopers coming from up the trail from his vantage point high above the Rim as they moved toward General Springs, which again was an important watering hole on the trail that led northwesterly across the Tonto Basin.

Natiotish thought his intelligence was good, because his people knew the lay of the land so intuitively. His mistake was overconfidence. He thought incorrectly, that he had the whole picture. What he did not know was that the minute he jumped the reservation the Captain Pierce the Indian Agent at San Carlos notified all of the army outposts to look out for the escaped renegades.

Word was sent to General Crook by a telegram, who just happened to be at nearby Fort Verde, indicating Chief Natiotish had jumped the reservation with seventy braves and was heading somewhere north near their position. Major Andrew Evans was immediately dispatched from

Fort Verde along with The Apache Kid who now at the age of 22, had been promoted to the rank of Sergeant of Scouts to intercept the renegades.

The Apache Scout Rowdy and Al Sieber, Chief of Scouts and the Kid, all happened to be at Fort Verde at that precise time when General Crook received the communication. Their orders were that they were to hunt down Natiotish, because of the killing spree, the minute he left the reservation and return them to the reservation. Unbeknown to Crook, Natiotish and his band already killed ten ranchers and all of the passengers and drivers of a Stagecoach they happened to come upon along their trek, to take the horses and any food they found.

The troops headed northeast from Fort Verde on the General Crook trail and figured they would intercept the fleeing Apaches somewhere at the top of the Mogollon Rim near General Springs.

Natiotish's observers had seen Major Andrew Evans and one company, but before he was joined by Lt. Chaffee at the end of the day on July 16th along with five companies of the 3rd and 6th Cavalry. Natiotish prepared an ambush on Evans and his troops for the following day by hiding in the rocks at a steep canyon that overlooked East Clear Creek. Lucky for the Army, his intelligence was nearly a day old. Meanwhile, Chaffee's own scouts, led by the Chief of Scouts Al Sieber and the Apache Kid, had spotted Natiotish, and figured that the Chief and his braves was under the impression that he would be springing a surprise attack.

Captain Adna Chaffee, and Lieutenant Evans concurred on a plan to outflank each of the Apaches positions overlooking the trail with two of his companies. When the Apaches attempted to spring their trap, the troopers would be behind them and would not allow them an escape rout.

On the morning of July 17th, As Evans moved into the Canyon that was over a thousand feet deep and seven hundred and fifty feet wide with two companies, Natotish struck from both sides of the canyon, believing that he was attacking the entire US Army force. Suddenly, each of his flanks was itself, under attack. The usual endgame for an Apache ambush had been for to simply pull back and fade away. This time, Natiotish found his exit route blocked. Chaffee had forced him to fight to the death or surrender and face the consequences.

When the dust settled Natiotish was thought to have been killed but his body was not found. Twenty-seven Apache bodies were found in the rocks and buried but that was less than half of the total Apache casualties. The rest of the Apache survivors were captured by the troops and only one trooper was killed in the skirmish.

This battle was known as *"The Battle of Big Dry Wash,"* and was the last outright battle fought between the Apaches and army regulars. It was also one of the few times that army soldiers fought and bested Apaches in an actual firefight battle but this was mainly because it was one of the few instances in which Apaches allowed themselves to be drawn into a conventional battle. They were the originators of guerrilla warfare.

The photo below of the location of the Battle of Big Dry Wash was found on the Hiking.com website

Captain Chaffee submitted his report of the battle to General Crook as soon as they returned to Fort Verde. Then Captain Chaffee and the scouts escorted the rest of the Apaches that survived the firefight back to the San Carlos Reservation to stand trial for their depravations.

General Crook read Captain Chaffee's report and when he finished made a statement posted in his memoirs that he would make history;

> *"It takes an Apache to catch an Apache."*

The Apache Kid had elevated himself to a level of trust that was unheard of for an Apache before the Battle of Dry Wash. General Crook called a meeting of the whole garrison and singled out the Kid as being the hero of the battle and that his keen scouting ability and knowledge of the surrounding territory surely saved the troops from a virtual massacre.

Below is a photo of the Apache Kid found in our National Archives that was taken right after the Battle of Dry Wash. The Apache Kid is pictured on the left and Hoscate, another of General Crook's scouts is pictured on the right.

Below is a newspaper article that appeared in the Phoenix City Herald on July 22nd 1882 covering the battle;

Apaches lose the Battle of Dry Wash

The remaining survivors of the White Mountain Apache Chiefs band of renegades, some 27 braves are on their way back to San Carlos. They effectively lost the firefight that took place at the Big Dry Wash on the Mogollon Rim. Settlers in the Tonto Basin are doubtless aware of the situation since several families suffered heavy casualties while Chief Natiotish and his renegades made their way through the Tonto Basin on their way up the Rim to a place called General Wash.

Below is of General George Crook. This picture of General Crook and, two of his Apache Scouts along with his mule ironically named "Apache" is courtesy of the Arizona Historical Society and was taken Circa 1885,

Chapter Ten

The Apache Kid was now the new Sergeant of Scouts, Al Sieber was the Chief of Scouts and along with Captain Adna Chaffee they all arrived back at San Carlos with the surviving prisoners from Natiotish's renegades who surrendered and survived the Battle of Dry Wash. A trial was held but all of the captives were released to live back on the reservation. The government was aware of the depravations happening on the reservation and took them into consideration when rendering an innocent decision.

Natiotish was a White Mountain Apache Chief but along with him was another Chief whose name has not been established. In any event the documentation below proves that he did exist. In the firefight that occurred at Cibecue Creek this other Chief jumped the reservation with Natiotish. He knew that nothing good was going to come from the firefight and no matter what, they would be blamed for the firefight and also since he stole an army horse he would surely be hung for horse stealing so again he decided to follow Natiotish.

When they arrived back at San Carlos the chief was one of the survivors of the firefight at the Battle of Big Dry wash. He was recognized by one of the scouts as being involved in the firefight at Cibecue Creek and charges were filed against him for horse stealing and murder. He was incarcerated when they arrived back at San Carlos until his arraignment.

Another newspaper article that appeared in the Phoenix City Herald on July 30th of 1882 that establishes his circumstances while he was being held as a prisoner. This article will give the reader a look at the state of mind of a person incarcerated with in his mind no hope for any leniency.

Incarcerated at the San Carlos

We are informed that a White Mountain Apache, incarcerated at San Carlos, on the charges of horse stealing and murder, feeling time hanging heavy upon his hands, asked that the cheerful influence of his wife and child might be permitted to pervade his lone cell. The request was granted and after remaining with him from 6 PM Tuesday until 4 AM Wednesday, he inflicted wounds upon them with a knife which resulted in their immediate deaths. Being still possessed with the devil he threatened death to anyone who should enter his cell. The guard being immediately doubled, and his detention assured, he for the time being, was left alone with his dead wife and child, until he could be further secured without endangering the lives of soldiers or guards in the accomplishment of the end in view. But "where there's a will there's a way," and the happy expedient of firing him was resorted to, which worked like a charm. Hay was inserted into the cell in quantities sufficient, when ignited to engage his individual attention and excite a desire to be somewhere else, and noting upon the impulse, he

improvised himself as a battering ram;
forced the door of his cell and passing
the portal, his light of life was snuffed by
several well directed bullets fired by
soldiers and scouts whose skins were
colored like his own.

In the month of April in the year 1883, almost a year after the incident involving the so called horse thief, Geronimo who again had given up and was living on the reservation decided to jump the reservation and took about fifty young unhappy braves with him. He could not get used to taking handouts from the white man for their survivorship and he loathed raising crops and being a farmer, according to Lieutenant Britton Davis's memoirs.

General Crook and his company of soldiers together with Al Sieber, The Apache Kid, scouts Rowdy and Messai as their scouts conducted a remarkable campaign that took them into the Sierra Madre Mountains in Old Mexico giving chase to Geronimo and his band of renegades.

In late May of 1883 Geronimo was tracked again to the Pa-Gotzin-Kay Plateau where he was resting and readying himself and his braves for a new campaign. The Apache Kid was sent into the camp to talk him into surrendering thereby avoiding the death of innocent people that were making their home there in peace. General Crook held no grudges against the Nameless ones that were a race loving people and besides they were living in another country. All he wanted was the outlaw.

The Kid delivered the message to Geronimo that General Crook was waiting below to talk with him. Geronimo agreed to talk with General Crook and after two days of negotiating the General finally convinced Geronimo to surrender and return to the San Carlos Reservation. By the end of June 1883 most of Geronimo's followers had returned to the reservation, but Geronimo himself didn't surrender until February of 1884.

The surrender of Geronimo taken in a field near Skeleton Canyon by the famous Tombstone photographer, C.S. Fly. General Crook is sitting second from the right and Geronimo is sitting third from the right. This picture is courtesy of Arizona State Archives, 97-2659.jpg.

This time Geronimo and his people settled at Turkey Creek, on the San Carlos Reservation, twenty miles south of Fort Apache. They started farming, but were unhappy and in May of 1885. Geronimo jumped the reservation again for the last time and this time he only had thirty young braves and their families that followed him this time. Most of his braves were tired of being on the run and going weeks without food so they decided to stay on the reservation and live in peace as farmers.

In the Spring of 1886 with the help of the Apache Kid, Tom Horn, Chatto as Interpreter and Al Sieber, Chief of Scouts with Lt. Britton Davis and Lt. Charles Gatewood conducted another *campaign* into the Sierra Madre Mountains looking for Geronimo. With the help of the Apache Kid, and Chatto as trailers, Lt Gatewood, who was in charge found that Geronimo and his followers were down to twenty braves and their families. They had run out of ammunition and had gone with out food for weeks so Geronimo agreed to surrender and met with General Crook at Canon De Los Embudos, which was just south of the Arizona border in the state of Sonora, Mexico.

However, on the return trip back to San Carlos after he and his followers were fed by the Army he stole a wagon full of supplies and broke out again. This time General Crook was furious. The General began to receive messages from his commander, General Phillip Sheridan, of the War Department that he considered insulting. General Sheridan seemed to imply that Crook was too soft on Geronimo. Therefore, General Crook asked to be relieved from his position. His resignation was accepted with regret. General Nelson Miles replaced General Crook and took command of the Arizona Territory.

Over the next five months General Miles put over 5000 troops in the field in his hunt for

Geronimo's tiny band of twenty warriors and about thirty women and children. Incredible exploits took place in the Sierra Madre Mountains, in Sonora, Mexico, then finally on September 4th of 1886, Geronimo surrendered for the last time at Skeleton Canyon in southeastern New Mexico near the town of Tombstone. It was not General Miles, however was not present when Geronimo surrendered, it was Lt. Charles B. Gatewood and the Chiricahua Apache scouts Martine and Kayitah. The Apache Kid was not present. He stayed behind with Lt. Britton Davis, because Geronimo hated the Kid. Geronimo specified that he would only surrender to Lt. Gatewood, because he trusted Gatewood.

Below is a photo found in our National Archives, was taken photographer C.S. Fly. Lt. Gatewood, is pictured second from the left. Martine is to Gatewood's right. Kayitah is standing to the right of the man sitting on the rock. Tom Horn is on the far right.

Chapter Eleven

Geronimo and his renegades arrived back at the San Carlos Reservation less than a week later. General Miles held a meeting with the Indian Agent Captain Pierce and most of his leaders the next morning after they arrived at the reservation.

In this meeting Miles thanked Lt. Gatewood for his amazing work in helping to bring Geronimo back to San Carlos. A nice thank you though, because the next morning Gatewood was ordered to an obscure outpost in Montana. Geronimo was an embarrassment to the Army. The next announcement from General Miles that had come down directly from the Secretary of War, General Sheridan was in essence, that the army no longer needed the services of the Apache Indian Scouts and that they would be released from their army duties and would be allowed to live in peace on the reservation but if they caused any trouble they would be sent to Florida like any other renegade.

This meeting was not taken well by the Indian Scouts, the white scouts and all of the army leaders. Lieutenant Britton Davis immediately turned in his resignation. He told General Miles he was appalled the Army's position in these matters. When he turned in his resignation he reminded General Miles that these Scouts had been sworn into the army and some of them only had a couple of years before they would be eligible for retirement. Davis's words fell on deaf ears.

Tom Horn, Clay Beauford and Al Sieber were enraged. Sieber spoke in behalf of the Apache scouts and plead his case to General Miles to let some of the scouts be offered transfers to the reservation police force and to keep some of them as scouts at least that way the scouts close to retirement would be able to retire with full pay at the end of their twenty years of government service. General Miles agreed to let ten of the scouts that Beauford and Sieber picked to move to the San Carlos Reservation Police squad.

The Apache scouts simply did not understand these rules. They openly displayed anger but Sieber and Beauford were able to convince the Apache Kid and Rowdy that the move to the reservation police would be a good move and that their time would bridge their service and allow them to complete their tour of twenty-year service and qualify for the retirement benefits. Most of the Scouts including Messai simply were livid and they refused to live on the reservation with the rest of the Chirichua, who hated them more than the renegades they helped capture, so they were put on the same train as Geronimo and sent to Florida, as prisoners of war.

The Kid and another trusted scout Rowdy did not understand what was happening but they both trusted Al Sieber and Clay Beauford and new the two of them had only good intentions for their welfare so they agreed to move to become reservation police and it wasn't long before the Kid and Rowdy both moved up in the ranks and became sergeants and enjoyed more rights and privileges as reservation police than they did as U.S. Army scouts.

The photo below was found in our National Archive of the train transporting Geronimo, the scouts and their families had stopped for a stretch break. Geronimo is 3rd from the right on the bottom row.

For six months after the deportation of Geronimo to Florida along with the other renegade Apaches, peace and quiet reigned at the San Carlos Reservation. This was only a lull before the storm, because some of the Apaches were not yet ready to accept the white man's customs and be assimilated with his society. A number of these Apaches gave government officials grave concern, the first was a young Apache named Nah-deiz-az.

Nah-deiz-az was an intelligent and neat person. He was only twenty-two years old when he got in trouble. He was a Yavapai Apache. He, his father and his mother survived the relocation and long cold trip from their homeland near Fort Verde to San Carlos, along with the rest of their nation. His mother died shortly after they established their new home at the reservation.

The young Apache brave was one of the first to adapt to farming. Settling on a fertile piece of ground on the Gila River, he fenced the land and became self-supporting, raising enough crops to feed himself, his father and a work horse, but the government objected to his occupying the land because it fell within the right-of-way of a proposed road.

On March 10, 1887, Nah-deiz-az was holding the plow handle with his father guiding the horse around and around the small field, breaking ground for spring planting. About noon he fed the horse, then he and his father began to prepare dinner in their wickieup which was situated a few steps from the fence that enclosed his property. He noticed Frank Porter, the reservation farm boss, come up to the fence on horseback. Porter shouted;

> "Nah-deiz-az! For the third and last time, I'm telling you that the government is going to use this land for a road."

In broken English, the young Apache explained how he had been brought there against his will, and the government was still not satisfied. Wiping tears from his eyes with a bandanna, he related his mother's sick condition while they made the long trip from their home near Fort

Verde to the San Carlos Apache Reservation and described her death shortly after completing the long hard journey;

> "That might be true, said Porter, but orders are orders. Get off this land and be damn quick about it! No, I stay, Nah-deiz-az responded. Porter said, then I have no choice but to report you to headquarters, as he turned around his horse and road away."

Porter reported to Captain Francis Pierce who was the Indian Agent in charge of the San Carlos Reservation at that time, who didn't believe the dispute too serious and thought that an army officer with authority could mend the breach that existed between the two and that the Indian would be willing to listen to reason and get off the land.

The person detailed to accompany Porter on this mission was Lieutenant Seward Mott, a soft spoken, diplomatic, and respected officer, whose name had become a tradition on the reservation.

Nah-deiz-az had started plowing again when he saw the two men come into sight. He walked into his home, picked up a pistol, cocked it and waited for them to arrive. Porter and Mott came closer, never suspecting that he had a weapon. As they were about to dismount, Nah-deiz-az fired at Porter. The bullet missed its mark, but it did hit and seriously wound Lieutenant Mott. As

Mott fell to the ground, Porter wheeled his horse and sped for his life to the reservation headquarters.

Captain Pierce was shocked with the report and rushed into an adjacent office and commanded Al Sieber, who was in charge of the reservation police force, who sent the Apache Kid to pursue the arrest of the young brave. The pursuers expected a battling, running chase, but they were surprised to find that Nah-deiz-az had not fled. He surrendered without resistance, gave up his pistol and expressed regret for mistakenly shooting Mott. Just where he obtained the pistol remained a mystery, except for the reservation scouts and police, the Apache living on the reservation were not allowed to own or carry side arms. They were only allowed a rifle to be used for hunting on the reservation.

While the arrest was being made, Doctor T.B. Davis, the post physician, rushed to give aid to the wounded officer and drove him in an ambulance to the hospital, where the medical staff labored to save his life. Despite a gallant effort from Davis and his staff, Lieutenant Mott died the next morning.

Authorities were more or less baffled as to what should be done with Nah-deiz-az in the matter of punishment. At one time crimes of this nature were subject to military court-martial but in 1885, but Congress passed a law stating that;

> *"All Indians committing crimes against the person or property of another for the following crimes, namely murder, manslaughter, rape, assault with intent to kill, arson, burglary and larceny within any Territory or State of the United States, and either within or without an Indian reservation, shall be subject therefore to the laws of such Territory or State relating to such crimes, and shall be tried therefore in the same courts and in the same manner and shall be subject to the same penalties as all other persons charged with commission of said crimes respectively."*

Arizona, still a United States territory, had an old court system. The judges were appointed by the President and usually came from the East. A judge was assigned to preside over the judicial district, which comprised of one or more counties. He was both federal and territorial judge and held court for both governments in the same courtroom. When sitting as a federal judge, the U.S, marshal and the U.S. attorney were his court officers, but when he sat as a territorial court the sheriff and the district attorney were his officers. On a number of occasions these judges got mixed up and defendants were tried in the wrong court. These judges also made up the Territorial Supreme Court, which decided cases that were appealed from the federal and territorial courts. A trial judge who had heard the evidence of a case which was appealed disqualified himself as a Supreme Court Justice in particular cases, but other judges, who knew nothing about the case, comprised the high tribunal.

Nah-deiz-az was held in the San Carlos guardhouse while legal minds studied the case to determine in which court he should be tried. It was decided that he violated federal law and that he should be tried in the Second Judicial District which was located in nearby Globe, Arizona.

Nah-deiz-az was brought before the Federal Judge W.W. Porter, no relation to Frank Porter, in May of 1887 for his arraignment and the trial was set for June of 1887. Federal Judge Porter was appointed by President Ulyses S. Grant. Judge Porter had a big nose and was easy to remember once you met him. After Nah-deiz-az declared he had no money for his defense, the court appointed a public defender as his counsel. Nah-deiz-az, through his attorney entered a plea of guilty at the trial, throwing himself at the mercy of the court. Judge Porter sentenced Nah-deiz-az to life in prison, the sentence to be served in the Yuma Territorial Prison, located three hundred miles southwest from Globe. The prisoner was immediately transported by deputies to the prison by train.

Enclosed in high adobe wall, the prison was located on Prison Hill, south and east of present day Yuma, Arizona on a granite bluff with the back of the prison facing the Colorado River. The dungeon block contained cells carved out of the rocky hill. Rings were imbedded in the solid rock floor where incorrigibles were chained.

Nah-deiz-az was confined in the main sell block, which housed prisoners with life sentences. The cells were made of stone, steel, and mortar with barren floors. The cells were equipped with six bunks each in tiers of three per side and were crowded to the point that prisoners could hardly move about. A canteen was placed in each cell for drinking water and a bucket was used for toilet facilities.

The sun's rays beating against the rocks often soared the temperature in the prison to over 120 degrees. Tuberculosis was prevalent, and prisoners could see prison guards carrying victims of the dreaded white plague to the prison graveyard. Conditions were horrifying to say the least.

Nah-deiz-az got a happy surprise, however, when the United States marshal received orders from the United States attorney general to transfer him to the Southern Illinois penitentiary located at Menard. The U.S. Court ruled that the Yuma prison was reserved for territorial prisoners. Judge Porter was ordered to send all future federal prisoners to the Ohio state prison, at Columbus, or the southern Illinois penitentiary, the two institutions which the United States had contracted with to incarcerate prisoners.

Chapter Twelve

Even before the courts and justice department settled all the technical points in the case of Nah-deiz-az, the Apache Kid who was now the most experienced and trusted police officer at San Carlos was called upon to investigate the murder of Lee Nasson, a freighter, whose body was found near the border of the San Carlos Reservation.

On April 10, 1888, Nasson was on his way to Globe with a cargo of goods, including several cases of whiskey consigned to a saloon, when he was attacked and killed by a band of renegades. His two wagons were burnt and the horses and whiskey were stolen.

The Kid found a portion of the unconsumed liquor at the scene upon his initial investigation, that was stashed in the bushes nearby the burnt wagons. The firewater looked tempting to him, but the honor and dignity attached to his position prohibited him from tasting the stuff. He suspected an Indian by the name of Captain Jack was the culprit. The Kid found out from witnesses that Captain Jack recently had been seen staggering drunk at the supply post.

Captain Jack was a jovial, good-natured brave, who did little jobs for the soldiers and asked travelers who came through the post for handouts. He wore a tattooed number on his forehead, SC1, which indicated that he was the first San Carlos Apache to be numbered. The number system again was instituted by General Crook as a means to identifying each Indian. In later years the numbering system was eliminated because the Native American Activists proclaimed the tattoo system was simply inhumane, so tags worn around the neck like army dog tags as they are called that were substituted for tattoos.

Captain Pierce, Al Sieber and the rest of the officials at the post were startled when they heard that Captain Jack could be implicated in the murder of the freighter. But when he was interrogated by the Kid he admitted being at the scene of the killing and helping drink the whiskey but denied any responsibility for the murder of Lee Nasson. He implicated Elcahn, Lacahor and Has-tin-tu-du-jay as his accomplices. We will not be hearing the last of Elcahn who was one nasty mean renegade.

The three Indians were arrested by the Apache Kid without resistance and were taken to Globe for trial, where Federal Judge Porter sentenced them to long terms in the Ohio State prison at Columbus.

Al Sieber and Captain Pierce were elated with the manner in which the Apache Kid caught the killers of Lee Nasson and they placed even more confidence and trust in him.

It was in the Kid's eighth enlistment, an enlistment at that time was generally one, two, three or four years. By now the Kid again had reached the rank of Sergeant in the reservation police squad and was considered the most trusted Apache leader at the reservation.

On May 11th 1888 the Kid was thrown into a no win situation that would change his life forever and lead to a court martial, a civil trial, a conviction and a prison sentence, his escape from justice, and the rest of life as a fugitive. Al Sieber, who was in charge of the reservation police force was ordered to accompany Captain Pierce on an inspection tour to Fort Apache. In preparations for his week's absence from the San Carlos post, Sieber called in his favorite scout and police sergeant the Apache Kid, and informed him that he would be acting chief of police during his absence.

This was an unprecedented honor conferred on him by his respected chief undoubtedly filled the young Indian's heard with great pride. For the moment, at least, Sieber's faith in him overwhelmed the conscience that sometimes nagged him with the thought that his alignment with the white man was a betrayal of his Apache blood.

The moment the reservation Indians heard that Captain Pierce was gone a large colony of them that were living on the San Carlos River about ten miles from the agency put on a big celebration. There was dancing, feasting, gambling and drinking.

Due to this massive celebration a series of disastrous events unfolded, as did so many disastrous events among the Apaches, with the brewing of Tiswin, a strong alcoholic beverage made out of fermented fruit or corn. Just like the Tiswin the old medicine man brewed and shared with the author.

Although federal law prohibited these merry makers from buying alcoholic drinks, they possessed plenty of liquid the ingredients to make their own concoction of Tiswin. Including the spirited alcoholic beverage mescal, which is made from the century plant; tulapai, that is also made from corn; and raisin jack, which is brewed from raisins, sugar and yeast.

Their gambling consisted of playing monte, which is a Mexican card game similar to poker. Their feast included such foods as beef, potatoes, beans, bread, coffee and sugar. Dancers expressed their feelings through the medium of a peculiar dance, stepped to the weird chants of monotonous thumping of tom-toms of the medicine men. The ceremony continued until dancers dropped from sheer exhaustion.

The party finally got a little too hilarious. First fist fights and hair-pulling contests broke out and when this information reached the military post at San Carlos, Lieutenant F. B. Fowler who was in charge during Captain Pierce's absence ordered the Apache Kid, the reservation police and scouts to go to the village and quell the disturbance. The Lieutenant acted in good faith, of course, but it turned out to be an ill-advised order to send a detail of Apache's to discipline a large assembly of their blood brothers.

The Kid, his scouts and police officers arrived at the camp and stopped on a knoll overlooking the camp. They were spotted by the partying Apache residents, who believed the Kid and his men came to do them harm. As the scouts started toward the gathering the celebrants began to yell at the leader, calling him by his Apache name, "*Haska-bay-nay-ntayl, U-ka-She! U-ka-she!*" which means Apache Kid go away.

The Apache Kid and his men did not swoop down on his people in wild commotion as they thought he might do, but they rode up in an orderly manner and dismounted. As he mingled in the crowd, looking for contraband, Apache maidens admired the handsome young brave, patted him on the cheeks and invited him to join the fun.

This camp just happened to be the camp of his own people and where his parents lived. Before he could go more than a couple of steps his mother ran up to him and informed him that something terrible had happened. She told him that two men were dead and that one of them was the Kid's father, Togo-de-chuz and the other dead man was the man who killed the kid's father, Gon-zizie. The Kid's friends killed Gon-zizie just before the Kid arrived at the village. The Kid's friends told him that Gon-zizie and his brother Rip confronted his father about being a spy and a drunken brawl Gon-zizie killed his father Togo-de-chuz and Gon-zizie's brother Rip escaped before they could kill him. The death of Gon-zizie was a terrible killing and according to the Apache code of honor, it became the duty of the Kid, who was the oldest son of Togo-de-chuz, to avenge his father's death by putting to death all involved with his murder.

After drinking for the better half of the day mourning his father's death the Kid went to the home of Rip who was Gon-zizie's brother and tried to arrest Old Rip for the murder of his father. A fight ensued and the Kid killed the old Indian in self- defense. Then he went back to his father's camp, where he joined the friends of his father in mourning by drinking Tiswin. The drunk lasted for several days.

When Captain Pierce and Al Sieber finally arrived back at the reservation they immediately heard about the incident and sent two Apache policemen to the camp where the Kid was staying to tell him he was to report to the reservation office immediately to explain the circumstances that caused the melee. They also wanted to know why the Kid abandoned his position at the reservation office, while they were gone and all he knew about the deaths of the three Apaches, who were killed at the melee.

The two policemen reported back to Al Sieber and Captain Pierce that the Kid said he would come in and give himself up in a few days after he had finished mourning the death of his father.

Finally, out of remorse and certainly hung-over the Kid and the eleven scouts arrived at the headquarters of the San Carlos Reservation on June 1st 1887. When they arrived they found that neither Al Seiber nor Captain Pierce was in a mood to deal generously with them. A crowd of Indians had gathered to witness the punishment that was to be handed out to the Kid, some were armed but when Captain Pierce ordered the scouts to disarm themselves, the Kid and his braves were the first to comply.

The Kid and his men laid their firearms on a table near Al Sieber's tent. Then Captain Pierce ordered the Kid and the others scouts to go to the guardhouse and be locked up until their fate was decided. They were about to comply when a shot was fired from the crowd but the shot was not by the Kid and soon it was a firefight with shots coming from everywhere on both the Indians and the Army side.

Below is a picture the guardhouse at San Carlos, courtesy of Arizona State Archives. 95-2823.jpg.

In the melee that followed, the disarmed Kid fled, Sieber's tent was shredded with bullets, and a massive 45-70 bullet smashed Sieber's left ankle. The wound left him crippled for the rest of his life. It has never been determined who fired the shot that struck Sieber, but it is known that neither the Kid nor the four policemen ordered to the guardhouse with him did the shooting. They all ran for cover, with the kid and his friends securing horses, and along with perhaps a dozen other Apaches, the all fled from the reservation in all directions heading for the wilderness. The Army acted swiftly, and soon two troops of the Fourth Cavalry were following the fugitives up the banks of the San Carlos River.

Telegrams were sent from the San Carlos Reservation to San Francisco which was the Army Headquarters Division of the Pacific, and to Washington, DC, as the Territories braced for another Apache outbreak.

Territorial newspapers in Arizona and New Mexico were quick to pick up the story and the Army began to feel the heat of irate editorials. For two weeks the renegade Apaches on the run, led the cavalry on a good chase, until, aided by fellow Indian police who had been scouts, the Kid and his band was located high in the Rincon Mountains. The troopers surprised the Indians and captured their mounts, saddles and equipment. The Kid and his gang escaped on foot into the rocky canyons and ravines but faced the prospect of survival without horses, with pressure from the army increasing.

Below is an article that appeared in the Phoenix Daily Herald on June 3rd 1887;

Indians on the loose

A dispatch was received here in Phoenix today from Fort McDowell by Sheriff A.J. Halbert that said as follows: Disputed information has been sent from the headquarters of the Department of the Army, several Apache police and scouts escaped resisting arrest and Al Sieber was shot in the melee. The Apache Kid and seventeen followers have left the San Carlos Reservation and were last located near Turnbull. The Army has troops on their trail but please notify settlers to be careful of their stock and not to go about single until the Apaches are back on the reservation.

Reported by E.J. Spaulding to the Phoenix Herald, Major 4th Cavalry

Below is another article that appeared in the Phoenix Daily Herald on June 19th 1887;

Points to the Escaped San Carlos Apaches

We are "broke up" over the Indian racket. Tow companies of the 10th cavalry are under orders to move at a moments notice and also the pack train horn. We will know in a few days whether there will be an Indian war or not. The Indians are reported to be in the Mount Trumbull area about fifteen miles from the San Carlos Reservation but I suppose you will have the news by telegraph.

This next newspaper article appeared in the Phoenix Daily Herald on June 20th 1887;

The Renegade Apaches from San Carlos

The weather has been so warm for the past two days that the troops are making little progress pursuing the escaped Apaches. A report from Wilcox last evening indicated the Indians were seen in the Sulphur Springs Valley last Wednesday in the vicinity of Henry Hooker's ranch, with the troops from Fort Grant in pursuit. Teamsters hauling freight at San Carlos report that the Indians on the reservation are impudent and aggressive and are apparently anxious to jump the reservation.

After some negotiation, the Kid got a message to General Miles stating that if the Army would recall the cavalry that he and his band would come in and surrender. General Miles called off the pursuit then on June 22nd 1887 eight of the kid's band surrendered and on June 25th 1887 the Kid along with seven other Apaches surrendered.

The article below appeared in the San Francisco Examiner on June 27th 1887;

Renegades Will Be Harshly Dealt

General Howard, head of the US Army in the West spoke this afternoon on the capture of the hostile Indians and said, "I am inclined to think these Apaches will be dealt with severely and with the extreme penalty of the law. Death may be indicted on some of them. A court martial will convene at once and will all likelihood be made up from nine to thirteen officers. Of Course the civil authorities may interfere, though it doesn't look like they are anxious to lend a hand. Since these Apaches were in the army as scouts or were reservation police, the army has the legal right to prosecute their own. Civilian authority does not take precedent in this case even so we will respect their position._

General Miles decided to try the Kid and his followers by a general army court martial, despite the fact that they did not, in all probability understand the charges pending against them. The trial was concluded in a day and to no surprise the men were found guilty of mutiny and desertion with each one being sentenced to death by firing squad. General Miles was very upset over the severity of the verdict, since no soldier was killed and only Sieber was injured, although again the injury left Sieber disabled and not able to work. Miles ordered the court to commute their sentences. The court reconvened on August 3rd 1887 and the convicted criminals were re-sentenced to life in prison.

General Miles was still not satisfied with the new verdict and reduced their sentences to ten years. The sentence was carried out at the San

Carlos guardhouse until such time as the Army decided where to send the prisoners. On January 23rd 1888, the powers to be decided to send the convicted prisoners to Alcatraz Island, California, rather than Leavenworth Military Prison and so the prisoners were taken were taken under heavy guard to Alcatraz to begin what would be a brief incarceration.

In reviewing the trial, the Judge Advocate's Office had become convinced that prejudice existed among the officers on the court martial, thus he felt they did not get a fair trial. On October 13th 1888 the secretary of War, William C. Endicott authorized the remission of the remainder of the sentences of the five prisoners, including the Apache Kid and by November they were all back in the stockade at the San Carlos Reservation.

Meanwhile, the Indian Rights Association concerned that the incarceration of Apaches as federal inmates in state prisons was the result of federal usurpation of territorial jurisdiction, so they filed suit on behalf of two of the incarcerated Apaches. The court agreed to the release not only of the two named Apaches in the suit but to the release of all the Apaches held as federal prisoners in Illinois and Ohio. Eleven murderers including the Apache Kid were returned to San Carlos as free men and the outrage in the Southwest was immeasurable.

Al Sieber thought it was a travesty of justice and together with the fact that he was now totally disabled due to the shot that destroyed his foot. Sieber held the Apache Kid responsible, even though he knew that the Kid did not do the shooting, so he started a personal vendetta to have the criminals arrested and this time he helped orchestrate state arrest warrants for the countless murders and other crimes committed in the Arizona Territory but especially for the Kid. An invalid was worse than a death sentence to a scout in the Old West.

Below is a picture taken in front of the Army Post at the San Carlos Reservation. John Clum is sitting in the middle, Tom Horn is wearing a white Shirt and Lt Gatewood is sitting next to John Clum. his photo found in the National Archives.

Chapter Thirteen

By the middle of October in 1889, Gila County Sheriff Glenn Reynolds had arrest warrants in hand for most of the freed Apaches including the Apache Kid. Everybody on the reservation knew where they were located so it was easy for the Sheriff to find the men, because they were celebrating their freedom. They were all arrested without incident.

The trial of the Apache Kid and the three other renegades for the charge of assault with intent to commit murder and the wounding of Al Sieber was set for October 25th 1889. It was again no surprise the four were found guilty and on October 30th 1889 each of them was sentenced to seven years in the Yuma Territorial Prison.

November 1st 1889 was chosen as the date to transport the Apache Kid along with seven other Apaches and one Mexican prisoner, Jesus Avota, to the nearest railhead in Casa Grande to catch the train to take them for incarceration at the Yuma Territorial prison notorious for its brutal living conditions also aptly called *"The Hell-Hole."*

The picture on the next page is of the convicted prisoners was taken at the San Carlos Reservation stockade just before they were transported to the Yuma Territorial Prison. The Apache Kid is the man standing second from the right wearing the wide brimmed hat. The Apache Kid was twenty-seven years old when this picture was taken.

This photo courtesy of the Arizona State Archives 96-3660.jpg

APACHE KID and his Red Devils in 1882. Kid is 2nd from right standing

Eugene Middleton was a local teamster and owned his own stagecoach. The army hired him to transport the prisoners to the railhead in Casa Grande and from there they would be transported by train the rest of the way to Yuma.

Al Sieber knew how dangerous these scouts were so he sent word to Sheriff Reynolds that he would send a squad of his scouts to escort them to the railhead. He told Sheriff Reynolds to wait until they arrive before setting out for Casa Grande. He was very disappointed when the Sheriff told him that his help was not needed.

Sheriff Glenn Reynolds figured it would take two days by stagecoach to go from Globe to Casa Grande because they had to go around the Pinal Mountains and the trail left a lot to be desired. He told Al Sieber in a telegram,

"I can take those Indians alone with a corncob and a lightning bug."

Confident in his superiority the sheriff only took one deputy with him, William "Hunkedory" Holmes. This was a serious error in judgment on the part of Sheriff Reynolds, because time would prove that the posse was indeed way too small for the job at hand.

The Riverside Stage Station. Photo is courtesy of the Arizona State Archives, 98-1612.jpg

According to the reports they did not encounter any problems the first day of the trip. According to Eugene Middleton the prisoners seemed very peaceful. He said they arrived at the Riverside Stage Station the first day in time for dinner. The prisoners were unloaded and still in shackles were taken to the dining room and all were fed a great dinner. After dinner the prisoners were shackled to in the building but had room to sleep. Everyone slept comfortable because the prisoners were far enough away from the lawmen and so they could all relax and enjoy a good night's sleep.

According to Jesse Avorta, during the night "The Kid," asked the stage driver Middleton for a cigarette, who gladly shared a smoke with "The Kid," a generous move that probably saved the stage drivers life, a fact that will be discussed later in this chapter.

Sheriff Reynolds and deputy Holmes were not so lucky on the second day of the journey. It turned bitter cold through the night due to a storm that occurred while they were asleep and they woke to four inches of snow on the ground on the morning of November 2nd 1889.

A few hours after leaving the Riverside Stage Station where they spent the night, just after they crossed over the Gila River and were making their ascent up the hill at a location called Ripsey Wash. The stagecoach started sliding because of the wet, snowing and sandy ground. At that point the sheriff took six of the shackled prisoners from inside the stage at the bottom of the steep wash on the trail to lessen the load.

As the little party trudged up the hill following behind the coach Bach-eonal, who is in front row and center of the picture on page 123, slipped free of his handcuffs, then Bach-eonal and Pash-laute, standing far left in the front row of the same picture on page 123, overpowered deputy sheriff Hunkdory Holmes during their escape. Due to their previous association with the army, the prisoners were not sure if they trusted the Apache Kid, who is standing second from the right in the back row of the picture on page 123 was still wearing his brass reservation tag on his left breast pocket when the others decided to free him. Deputy Hunkydory Holmes died of a heart attack during the daring escape before being shot by El-Cahn. Sheriff Glenn Reynolds was killed during the firefight by Hoscate, standing second from the left, Sayes, is standing third from the left.

According to Middleton's report the escaped prisoners grasped the sheriff who was walking in front of them while two other Indians wheeled upon Deputy Holmes who was walking behind the prisoners. Holmes though very brave suffered from a heart condition and when the trouble started he fell backwards as his pistol was wrenched from him by Pashlaute, standing far right next to the Apache Kid. Knowing his fait caused him to have a major heart attack and he died right on the spot before Pashlaute could finish him off.

It was always better to kill the prisoner rather than him die of fright because the Apaches believed taking a life in battle gave them power that was taken by the death of an enemy. The harder the death the more power the brave would receive from the gods. Sheriff Reynolds wrestled with Pash-laute to the ground after seeing his deputy lying dead on the ground and in the process of the struggle was shot in the neck. Making sure Holmes was dead Pash-laute put a bullet in Holmes chest while he lay lifeless on the cold soggy ground.

Eugene Middleton lived, even though he was severely wounded. He reported that he stopped the stage when he heard the commotion behind him and with a pistol in hand held the two prisoners that were left in his care at gun point. One of the prisoners, the Kid shouted in good clear English,

> *"Me be good Indian. We will stay*
> *seated, please don't shoot us."*

The scene of the tragedy that occurred behind the stagecoach driver and down the wash was not visible from the stage and the pistol shots were thought by Middleton to have been fired by the Sheriff or the Deputy. A moment later he was better informed of the situation when Jesus Avota, the Mexican prisoner ran up to the coach seeking his own safety, just as Pash-laute, hiding from behind the coach fired at the Middleton with the sheriff's rifle.

The four horses that were pulling the stage bolted from the scene when Middleton dropped the reins and fell to the sand with a bullet through the cheek, neck and left side of his body. The Indians rolled him over searching for valuables and cartridges. Fully conscious he felt the muzzle of a rifle against his temple. Then as Hoscate was about to make sure of Middleton was dead, the Kid, according to the report by Middleton, saved his life by saying,

"Save the cartridges, he is dead anyway."

Middleton reported that he saw the Kid take money from the Sheriff's body along with a pocket watch and his pistol, which were both marked with his name. The Mexican prisoner, Jesus Avota said he hid in the bushes and watched the Apaches molest the bodies and take all of their guns and ammunition. After they left Middleton escaped, suffering a serious gunshot wound to his neck and jaw, somehow made his way to the nearby town of Florence, where he reported the incident. He received a pardon from the Territorial Governor for trying to thwart the incident.

Leaving Middleton and freeing up the rest of the captives Middleton *"played possum,"* the Apaches unshackled themselves, took their commitment papers from the sheriff's pocket, tore them up, gave a whoop of joy and left the scene. When all was still, Middleton, horribly wounded was able to stagger to his feet and went to seek help. He found that Holmes body had not been molested, but the Sheriff Reynolds face had been terribly jabbed and cut by the muzzle of the gun and his forehead had been smashed.

It was not until the following morning that Middleton managed to drag himself back to the Riverside Way Station which was five miles away to get help for his wounds and to notify authorities about the disaster.

Below is a photo of a Concord Coach like the one used by the teamster Eugene Middleton.

Below are two photos used with permission from Hiking.com. The first one is Ripsey Wash, from where the coach started to head up the grade to the Riverside Stage Station.

The picture on the next page shows the steep incline of the road leading from Ripsey Wash up the mountain

side with the Riverside Stagecoach Station

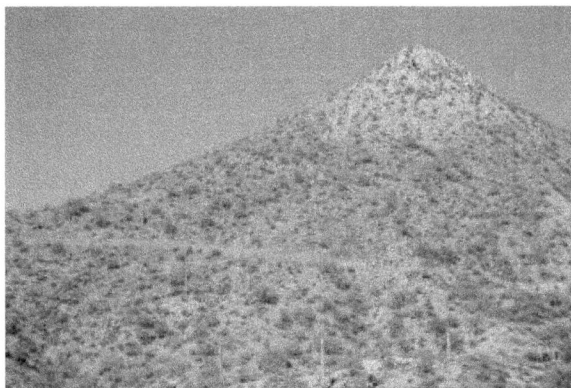

Following below and on the next page is the first article in a series that appeared in the Phoenix City Herald on November 2nd, 1889, regarding the murder of Sheriff Glenn Reynolds and Deputy Sheriff Hunkedory Holmes;

Sheriff of Gila County Murdered

Florence Arizona, Nov 2nd: Today, as Sheriff Reynolds, of Gila County, was on his way to the penitentiary at Yuma, with eight Indians and one Mexican, who had all been convicted of various crimes at the late session of the District Court at Globe, Arizona. The convicts made an attack on him and the guards, when about four miles south of Riverside, on the Gila River. They killed Sheriff Reynolds and one of the guards, all the prisoners escaping. A posse has gone out to bring in the dead bodies, much excitement prevails. The prisoners will undoubtedly be soon overtaken and captured.

A posse from Globe immediately started on the trail of the fugitives after but soon had to return because of the continuing severe snowstorm. The escaped Indians had struck up the Gila River to the mouth of the San Pedro River near the site of the town of Hayden and then on to San Carlos for whatever reason.

Below and following on the next page is another newspaper article in the series that was published in the Phoenix City Herald on November 3rd 1889. This article provides a little more information about the crime;

The Murdered Sheriff

Charles T. Martin, recorder of Gila County, says then Sheriff Reynolds reached the long hill coming out of Ripsey Wash, four miles from Riverside, last Saturday, he unshackled six of the eight Indians so that they could walk up the hill.

They were still handcuffed together, two and two. Stage driver Middleton remained on the driver's box, with two Indians in the stage, the Mexican prisoner walking just behind the stage, followed by Sheriff Reynolds then came along the six Indians, followed by Deputy Sheriff Holmes.

Jesus Avota, the Mexican prisoner, said he heard a yell behind him. Upon looking around he saw that two of the Indians had hold of Reynolds and two had hold of Holmes. The Mexican ran up to the stage and asked Middleton to let him in before he was killed. All they while shots were heard behind and the two Indians made an attempt to get out of the stage but Middleton with his pistol made them stay in the stage. While Middleton was looking back leaning from the driver's seat he was shot in the right cheek, the ball ranging down the side of his neck, knocking him of the stage. He remained in a half conscious condition until the Indians had gone, and then he walked back to Riverside, but there was no one there to pursue the murderers.

Avota said he took a horse from the team that the Indians left and started towards Florence, but being bucked off three or four times, became disgusted with the wild horse and went on ahead on foot. He said he realized the Indians left the horse because they also tried to ride it but were also successful.

The Indians rifled through the dead men's pockets. Then they rode off on the four horses. Reynolds was shot in the face and shoulder, evidently from his own gun. Holmes was shot in the head with a single ball but reportedly suffered from a heart condition and suffered a heart attack from all the excitement.

The next article appeared on November 4th 1889 in the Phoenix City Herald and is Middleton's version of the melee;

The Killing of Sheriff Reynolds
The following is the stage driver's account to the Tucson Daily Star of the killing of Sheriff Reynolds and his

deputy near Riverside, by eight escaping Indians and one Mexican prisoner, as noted in a special to Saturday's Phoenix City Hearld: "The party was ascending the long sandy pass west of Riverside, Sheriff Reynolds and Deputy Holmes were walking behind the stagecoach. The prisoners were all in the coach. The Mexican was sitting in the box with the driver, Eugene Middleton, pulled Middleton's six shooter when he turned to see the commotion and shot me. Middleton went on to say he fell of the stage and was unconscious and remembered nothing more that occurred until he came to and found Reynolds and Holmes dead on the ground near him. The prisoners and the stage were gone."

Middleton said, "I was able to walk back four miles to Riverside and announced the tragedy. He went on to say, I was shot in the neck and the ball came out of my cheek, leaving an ugly wound and I had a scalp wound on my head and I was bleeding pretty bad."

The opinion prevails that Reynolds and Holmes were ambushed, as they carried a shotgun and a Winchester rifle, 30/30 caliber lever action, again because it was cold and they had their duster's buttoned which did not allow them to get to their pistols when they were attacked by the prisoners.

Orders were issued for troops from Forts Apache, Lowell, McDowell, Grand and San Carlos to take the field in pursuit. The troops left San Carlos at 1 *o'clock Saturday under the command of Lt. Watson, an experienced Indian trailer.*

The next article following the pursuit appeared again in the Phoenix City Herald on Nov 5th 1889;

Funeral of Murdered Officers

Globe, Nov 5: The funeral of Sheriff Reynolds and Deputy W. A. "Hunkydory" Holmes, the victims of the Riverside tragedy, occurred yesterday and all Globe was in mourning, all business houses being closed. The services were conducted under the auspices of the Masonic and Odd Fellow's Lodges. Information just received from San Carlos says that the trail of the escaped Indians led right up to the San Pedro River, thence east into the mountains.

The band was separated but all were still on foot. Three of them wore shoes and five wore moccasins, all armed, halve with Winchester rifles and the other half with pistols. Lieutenant Welder and party are in close pursuit. The Apache Kid and Washlantah were seen yesterday on the San Carlos River four miles from the agency and an unsuccessful attempt was made to capture them. Their squaws are missing. Signal fires have been seen in the Pinal and Saddle Mountains.

On the next page are pictures of the two slain officers also found in our

- 138 -

National Archives. Gila County Sheriff Glenn Reynolds is left and Deputy Hunkedory Holmes is on the right.

The following is an article that appeared in the Tucson Daily Star on November 6th 1889;

The Indians Caught

Tucson, November 6: The eight Indian slayers of Sheriff Reynolds are reported captured Monday afternoon by United States Army troops on the San Pedro River. A freshly killed cow betrayed them.

The Apache Kid was not caught and the first article indicates he got away. The article above was incorrect. The Kid escaped alone and made his way through Skeleton Canyon and to freedom in the Sierra Madre Mountains.

It was also reported that the wife of a rancher named Cunningham upon hearing of the escape of the Apaches and hearing that his ranch was on the way they were going, died of a heart attack from fright. When they arrived *back at San Carlos most of the renegades were killed by Indian Scouts and Reservation Police when they were served arrest warrants.*

The head of the escaped outlaw Pash-laute was cut off when he was killed and the Indian police and took the head to the Indian Agency headquarters at San Carlos in order to give full assurance of his death. Hoscalte and Sayes were severely wounded when they were captured and both were tried and sentenced to life in the Yuma Territorial Prison where again they died of Tuberculosis. TB or "The Coughing Sickness," as it was called by the Indians was responsible for most of the deaths of the Native American population across our country. It was highly contagious and flourished in the hot dry climate of the Southwest.

It was spread by singing, coughing and sneezing. Because of these factors and the lifestyle of these Native Americans, living in Tee Pees, Wickieups and Hogans with little or no air movement the disease spread rapidly when it was introduced in an Indian village. John Clum stated to friends that in one of the reports he read on his way to San Carlos, that the army did their best to introduce several diseases including to the Indians in hopes that the diseases would help them exterminate their enemies.

On the next page are two pictures of the Yuma Territorial Prison that was used to house prisoners until 1908 when the new Arizona State prison was completed in Florence, Arizona. The first picture details the construction of the prison cells. The reader can see from the pictures that this prison was well fortified, the cells are built outside.

The picture below was taken from a guard tower and shows the main dinning building and part of the yard at the old Territorial Prison in Yuma. This picture is also courtesy of Arizona State Archives 98-6970.jpg

Chapter Fourteen

By a strange course of events, The Apache Kid was no longer an admired, honored scout and trusted policeman, but a fugitive with a price of $5000 on his head. It is widely believed that the Kid used the San Simon Valley in Southern Arizona and Skeleton Canyon in Southwestern New Mexico to make his escapes back and forth from the USA to Mexico. His plan was to hideout with the Naiche and Nameless ones living in peace at Pa-Gotzin-Kay plateau in the Sierra Madre Mountains of northern Sonora, Mexico at least until the heat died down.

At this point because of the escape incident his life of peace was over for good. He would never see his wife or children again and now he was hated not only by his own people but everyone that lived in the Territory.

The following articles follow the search for the Kid and his followers. This one appeared in the Phoenix City Herald on July 3rd 1890;

Can Cross the Mexican Border

An agreement has been entered by Secretary of State Blaine and Mexican Minister, Romero providing for the reciprocal crossing of the International boundary line by troops of the United States and Mexico while in close pursuit of hostile Indians. Under this agreement a crossing shall only occur in unpopulated or desert parts of the border.

The next article pertaining to the Kid gang was published in the Globe Tribune on July 16th 1890;

Indian or White Murders

Information was received here last night of the discovery of the dead body of Edward Baker at his cabin in the Sierra Ancha Mountains, forty miles north of Globe. He is supposed to have been murdered on the 14th of July. Some doubts are expressed as to whether the deed was committed by Apaches or white rustlers, but the fact of the body having been mutilated about the head points to a killing by Indians. A number of horses were stolen and the cabin was looted. Citizens from Salt River and Sheriff Thompson with a posse left yesterday for the scene of the tragedy. The troops and scouts from San Carlos and surrounding army posts are also in route.

The next article appeared in the Tucson Daily Star on July 18th 1890. It further follows the search for the Kid and his followers;

Got One More Indian Murderer

Wilcox Arizona July 18-News has just been received here that Lieutenant Mackey and his scouts, while in battle this afternoon with the Kid gang, in the Sierra Anchas mountains killed Wahlantha. He is the third member of the Kid gang who has gone to the happy hunting ground since that lamentable occurrence and since which time they have been roaming over the country murdering and plundering and were doubtless the ones who killed Dr. James Hardie who was riding on a stage that was attacked by the Kid Gang.

The officers and scouts are following their trail closely and it is though they will soon capture the Kid and the remainder of his followers.

Wahlantha's head was sent to the nearest post for identification. He is one of the Indians who killed Sheriff Reynolds last fall and is supposed that it was he, with the Kid gang who murdered Dr. Hardie a short time ago in Rucker canyon.

This next article further informs us of the manhunt for the remainder of the Kid gang and appeared in the Tucson Daily Star on July 21st 1890;

Glenn Reynolds Murderers

Tucson, July 21- It is now definitely known that the eight Apache prisoners under the Kid, who murdered Sheriff Reynolds and the deputy and then escaped, that all save three have been killed. Kid and two others are still at large. Detachments of troops from all the forts are out with hopes of intercepting them. Lieutenant Michael with his scouts has been in pursuit of them since his fight last Friday, in which one of the renegades, Wahlantha was killed. Three White Mountain Apache renegades came in the surrendered to the troops. They confirm the report that all but three of the Kid gang has been

- 144 -

killed.

After six of the Kid's companions were captured and two were hung (the other four committed suicide by strangling each other with their loin cloths while in their cells the morning before their execution), the Kid went on the warpath and a murder rampage, killing several settlers. He attacked a prairie schooner in which a woman, her young son and an infant son were traveling to meet the woman's husband.

The next article appeared in the Globe Tribune on July 26th 1890 and further follows the pursuit of the remainder of the Kid Gang;

Another Apache Killed
Globe, Arizona July 26th-Sayes, the Apache renegade wounded in a fight with military on Ash Creek on July 17th was captured yesterday by chief Antonio's men on the San Carlos River and has been placed in a military guard house on the reservation. Sayes is on of Kid's band who murdered Sheriff Reynolds and Deputy Holmes this past November.

Sayes had in his possession Sheriff Reynolds rifle which he says, Poshlantah, who was killed on the 17th had given it to him. This leaves only the Kid himself and Tonto Basin Sixty alive out of the party of eight convicts who participated in the murder of Sheriff Reynolds. It is reported that Tonto Basin Sixty has also been killed but the report cannot be verified. Sayes boasts of having killed several white men during their escape. He will be tried in Pinal County for the murder of Sheriff Reynolds and his deputy.

Below and on the next page is another article found by the author relating to the Apache Kid, that appeared in the Phoenix City Hearld on August 16th of 1890 and it presents more evidence about the Kid's accomplice Sayes being captured;

Hardie's Murderers

San Carlos, A.T. August 16th- The information given by the captured scout, Sayes and the other renegade, Curley, who were both closely questioned on the within subject, is about the name. Sayes one of the convicts who murdered Sheriff Reynolds and escaped from the civil authorities in November last, admitted that he was one of the three bucks present at the murder of Mr. Hardie in Rucker Canyon, the other two being, Wash-tan-tah (Killed on July 17th) and the Kid still at large. After shooting Hardie, Sayes says Kid and Wash-tan-tah robbed him, taking very little money, which Kid gave his squaw, who was also present at the time of the killing.

He then took Hardie's watch and beat the inside works out against a rock, then gave the case to Wash-tan-tah who

cut it in strips for rings and other rude ornaments. A small watch chain- the one sent herewith- was found near Wash-tan-tah's body, on the 17th after the fight. This is the information I have been able to elicit from the prisoner. Should the Kid be captured, which is highly unlikely, as our efforts have, not been relaxed, an attempt will be made to get further information on this subject letter.
Lewis Johnson,
Captain 23rd infantry- Lieutenant Colonel
San Carlos Post Commander

The Kid stopped the covered wagon, shot the woman and boy to death but oddly spared the infant. This crime incensed the military and the civilian population and hundreds set out to hunt down the killer Indian. At this point the military and the bounty hunters that were on his trail gave him a new name, "The Ghost in the Desert," because he would appear to do his bad deeds and disappear just as quick as he appeared leaving no sign or tracks to be followed. He usually attacked his victims without them even knowing he was there then he would slip away in the darkness or even in broad daylight.

Below is an article about another incident believed to be the work of the Kid gang near Skeleton Canyon in Southwestern New Mexico that appeared in the Phoenix City Herald newspaper on August 23rd of 1890;

More Apache Murders

Deming, New Mexico, August 23rd-Parties who arrived yesterday from the Tehachita mountains eighty miles south of here, confirmed the reported murder by Apaches of three miners named Alf Williams, Carl E. Herman and Peter Riggs within the past week. Military authorities say it was the work of two Indians believed to be what is left of the Kid gang who appeared to be on their way to Mexico. Citizens report that there were five in the party and that two miners survived. Two army detachments are following their trail.

There was no information available via newspaper articles about the Kid and his remaining partner in crime other than the other Apache had been identified as Chiquito.

The below is the last known photo of the Apache Kid, in the middle, to his right is Rowdy and Messai is pictured on his left. This picture was taken by C. S. Fly the famous Tombstone photographer and is courtesy of the Arizona State Archives 97-2603e.jpg;

Then on September 15th of 1890 the article below appeared in the Phoenix City Herald concerning the Kid gang;

Kid, The Renegade

One of the Last of the Reynolds Indian Murderers is Captured

Tucson, Arizona, Sept 15th- A private dispatch to San Carlos announces that Chiquito, Father-in-law of the renegade Indian Kid, has surrendered to John Forrester, a white man living with an Apache squaw on his ranch at the mouth of Aravaipa Canyon. Chiquito was a peaceable Indian till this spring, when he joined the band of renegades under the Kid, after the murder of Sheriff Reynolds although he was not implicated in the murders of the sheriff and his deputy.

A detachment of soldiers passed through this city this very afternoon in hot pursuit of the Kid himself believed to be the only survivor of his gang of cutthroats.

Another report that arrived from San Carlos was that a squaw arrived there today and claimed to have been with the Kid. She says she left the Kid at 11 o'clock the previous night at a point near Black Rock, at the northeast corner of Turnbull Mountain. Also she said that she and the Kid separated from a party traveling from Mexico, consisting of the Kid, his squaw and his son.

Chiquito and the Apache Kid had a disagreement. Chiquito told the Kid that he was going back to Aravaipa to give himself up as he was tired of fighting. He said he advised the Kid not to kill anymore white men.

The Kid told the squaw that troops were in pursuit and he told her he could not care for her any longer and she said he told her to take care of herself so he gave her his pony named Buckskin.

According to the captured squaw, the Kid left in greatly reduced circumstances with a bay pony no saddle, one carbine and one belt of ammo. The squaw stated that she was captured by Kid from another band of renegades led by Masseon Cibicu, a White Mountain Apache and she wanted to go home.

News has been received that there are troops in pursuit of Kid from Fort Grant, Fort Thomas and San Carlos. The troop from San Carlos came up to him at the second canyon northeast of Turnbull Mountain. In the hope of his capture a reward of $1500 has been offered.

The next article follows the chase of the Kid and it appeared again in the Phoenix City Herald on September 27th 1890. At first it was thought this may not have been the Kid gang but after the army investigated it appears it was the Kid gang;

Depredating Indians
Hillsboro, N.M. Sept 27- Yesterday a Mexican who resides on a ranch two-miles northeast of the town came and

*reported that a band of Apaches near
his ranch was rounding up ponies.
Citizens to the number of thirty armed
and started in pursuit. Up to a late hour
no news was received at Hermosa,
thirty miles north of Hillsboro. Signal
lights were seen nightly in the
mountains. It was reported the Apaches
make raids in the valley, kill cattle and
run off horses. Troops of the 11th
infantry is expected here from Fort
Bayard and a troop of cavalry that has
been in Chloride where two men were
murdered on September 17th will arrive
this morning when the forces will
consolidate and join in the pursuit.*

A scout by the name of Dupont while on the
Kid's trail abruptly came across the Kid on a trail
in the Catalina Mountains sometime in late
September of 1890. Both men had single shot
rifles, paused and stared at each other. Neither
wanted to waste one shot and be at the mercy of
the other so they dismounted, sat on rocks
through the long hot day, glaring at each other
while the sun beat down upon them. At dusk, the
Kid stood up and grunted, *"Me leaving."* With that
the killer mounted his horse and rode off while
Dupont heaved a heavy sigh of relief.

The next article about the Kid appeared again
in the Phoenix City Herald on October 2nd 1890;

Troops on the Trail of the Renegades
*Several companies of cavalry have
now been out after the renegade
Apaches about two weeks but Not an*

Indian has been captured though fresh crimes are being reported. The latest from the Black Range country, which has been their rondezvous in every outbreak for years along with the Sierra Madre Mountains in Mexico is that two bodies of miners were found day before yesterday riddled with bullets and their scalps were taken. The people to the south are much excited and if the government does

not put a stop to these annual raids of a few renegades it is stated they will organize themselves into companies and exterminate savages.

Below is a picture taken by C.S. Fly, courtesy of the Arizona State Archives 98-0379.jpg. Lieutenant Charles Gatewood and his company, found in our National archives, in pursuit of the Apache Kid.

The above photo of Lt. Gatewood and his company of the U.S. Army Cavalry and scouts was found in our National Archives, and is public domain. Lt. Charles Gatewood is riding a horse in the middle of the picture, looking at the horizon through a pair of binoculars. The company was hot on the trail, in pursuit of the Apache Kid. The two scouts that are following the trail are Martine pictured on the left and Kayitah pictured on the right. Tom Horn is pictured on the right riding a horse. I was unable to identify the other three Apache Scouts that appear in this photo.

Another article I found that is related to the Kid appeared in the Phoenix City Herald on October 6th of 1890;

Kid Killing Promiscuously

Tucson, Arizona October 6th- Information was received here this morning that the Kid in the mountains near Fort Thomas had shot a young White Mountain Apache. He said the whites and Indians had killed all his friends and he wanted therefore to kill everybody he met. An unconfirmed telegram from San Carlos states that six Apache scouts have been killed by the Kid.

For several years the Kid said he and a small band of renegade Apache followers raided ranches and freight lines throughout New Mexico, Arizona and Northern Mexico, hiding out in the Mexican Sierra Madre Mountains. The price of $5000 was still placed on the Apache Kid's head but no one ever claimed the reward. Edward A. Clark, who had been the partner of Bill Diehl, whose ranch was the first one the Kid raided on his way to Mexico, continued *to live on the ranch located about ten miles north of Skeleton Canyon.*

The Kid raided the ranch several times to obtain food and new mounts. According to Clark the last attack occurred in the spring of 1894 when the Kid and his men surrounded the ranch house and lay siege to James Clark, his new partner, John Scanlon and a visiting Englishman named John Mercer.

When night fell, Clark slipped out of the house and worked his way toward the corral where he saw two Indians leading away his favorite horse. He fired two shots in the dark toward the moving shadows then sat quietly until dawn. Then right at dawn he found the body of a squaw and a trail of blood leading away from the spot of the woman's body. Clark followed the trail of blood but it ended in the rocks of the high hills. "It was the Kid all right," Clark later claimed, "He probably crawled away to die somewhere in those hills." This theory proved not to be accurate.

The next news following the Kid plight was not until March 30th of 1891. The Apache Kid was still on the lamb and his father-in-law, Chief Eskimenzin was being held with three other Apaches for helping the Apache Kid. This article again appeared in the Phoenix City Herald;

Trouble at San Carlos
Willcox, AZ A.T. March 30- Nine Renegade Apaches have been arrested

within the last 48 hours and placed in irons at San Carlos under guard. Among the prisoners captured is old Chief Eskiminzen. Five of the prisoners are charged with the murder of a white miner several years ago, Old Chief Eskiminzen and the other three were apprehended for giving aid to "Kid" the notorious renegade and murderer. Eskiminzen is the father-in-law of the "Kid." All of the "Kid's" close and open companions in crime have been killed but he was said to have appeared last week within seven miles of the San Carlos Reservation. Troops were immediately sent in pursuit of him six days ago, up to yesterday nothing had been heard from them.

To add to the already intolerable living conditions at San Carlos due to drought and pestilence, the article below from the School Superintendent at San Carlos to the Bureau of Indian Affairs talks about a major flood caused by a serious rain storm at San Carlos that had been suffering a drought for two years. This article appeared in the Phoenix City Herald on April 9th 1891. It further explains why the Apaches were jumping off the reservation in droves and joining up with the Kid;

San Carlos Wards

Shakespeare, MaCauly and Irving could not Adequately Portray their Misery, Says Agent Lemmon, without much squeezing either.

The following picture of Indian destitution is sent officially from San Carlos, by way of Washington and appeared in the St. Louis Globe Democrat Washington D.C., April 9th- The Indian Bureau is in receipt of a letter from Theodore G. Lemmon, Superintendent of the Indian School at the San Carlos Reservation, in which he gives an account of the devastation caused by the recent flood in the Gila Valley. He went on to explain that many of the adobe buildings on the reservation were ruined by the storm, and the irrigation ditches were almost wholly destroyed. Not only were buildings belonging to the agency washed away, but faming implements and household goods also went down the river with flood. According to Lemmon, "Some of these Indians are now without homes, food and hunger is a telling sign on their faces. He went on to say, "Mothers want to put their babies in school to get something to eat, as we feed the school students when they spend the day with us, as they must be fed and they must be moved, or they will move off the reservation to feed themselves and the government will have them to kill."

Evidently the Indians are growing impatient over their prospects and Lemmon warns the department that there are just three possibilities affecting them temporarily.

He said, "They must be fed by provisions from somewhere else; in case they are not, they must become renegades and live by stealing cattle and plunder or they will die of famine and its consequences."

He says it is impossible to conceive the devastation caused by the flood. "You will never know the damage to those wild and

reckless people."

He goes on to explain to the Commissioner of Indian Affairs, "Had I Shakespeare's knowledge of English words, Macauley's power with the English language and Irving's descriptive abilities, and most studied application of all would leave you without and adequate conception of the condition here. Indians here on the grounds have no idea of the condition here and they have no conception as yet of their real condition; few white people more than the most meager conception. Something awful has transpired, a terrible flood has come and gone only a few have gotten over the stupefaction. With nowhere to turn Superintendent Lemmon appealed to the department for immediate relief for the distressed tribes.

Then on April the 15th 1891, Lemmon after not getting a timely response from the BIA decided to send a stronger communication depicting the devastation and misery at San Carlos. This article appeared in the Phoenix City Herald;

San Carlos conditions are Intolerable

San Carlos Agent Lemmon sends Washington an appalling description of

- 157 -

misery at his agency. The greatest writers of modern times, he says could adequately not tell the Indians wretchedness there impending. This assertion is what leads to distrust Agent Lemmon. It must be a mighty tough case that neither Shakespeare, Macauley nor Washington Irving could tackle successfully.

Then again neither the Silver Belt, of Globe nor the Solmonville Bulletin has heard of this deplorable destitution. The Kid and his renegade followers are said to be hovering about San Carlos and will feed their reservation brethren. Agent Lemmon himself says, "The Indians here on the ground have no conception as yet to their real condition." Why did Agent Lemmon call the Secretary of War, Proctor's attention to this grace situation when he recently passed through that country? Is the main question.

We hope the Indians are not in want. Even a hungry yellow dog is to us an object of pity. We fear Agent Lemmon has permitted his imaginative faculty to soar aloft, regardless of literal veracity. In other word's it looks very much as thought the agent's lively fancy were giving Commissioner Morgan what is known as "Guff."

On December the 12th 1895 the Kid and his band of renegades penned up three white men on a hillside twenty miles southeast of the San Bernadino Ranch north of Benson, Arizona. One of the men was Gus Mickey, who later became chairman of the Board of supervisors of Cochise County, Arizona and a prosperous merchant in Bisbee. Gus reported that he saw the Apaches and recognized the Kid from wanted posters but he said he did not get a clear shot at the renegade.

The other two men that were local cowboys Jack Bridger and Buck Robinson were hired by a local rancher to round up cattle near Skeleton Canyon to send to market. Buck and Jack were called to a spot by a cowboy by the name of Mickey Mills, who found a steer that had been killed by the Indians. When the trio got close to the dead animal one of the killers were still there, Bridger swiftly raised his rifle, shot and killed the Indian who was so busy butchering the animal he did not hear the men sneak up on him.

Immediately after shooting the Indian they found themselves surrounded by no less than twelve braves led by *"The Apache Kid."* The white men were behind a clump of rocks in making a rather insecure fortification. One of the attacking Apache party was the notorious "Big Foot," whose moccasin tracks, it was claimed, measured fourteen inches in length.

A siege continued for several hours, and the party behind the rocks had begun to reel relative security, when a shot knocked a corncob pipe from Buck's mouth. Jack Bridger, laughing at the occurrence, leaned forward, possibly exposing himself, and received a shot through the head. Only a few minutes later, Robinson fell back killed in the same manner.

Then it was Mickey Mills established a marathon record and beat an Apache Indian at running. He struck the trail for camp in the bottom of a sandy gorge in which some water however, was flowing. At the first bend, he sprang behind a boulder on the side of the canyon and struck away a right angle, while the Indians kept running down the canyon thinking him still ahead, on the well trodden trail. Mickey had been cut off from his horse, so flight on foot was his only means of escape and he made it safely to the Milt Hall ranch about two miles from the skirmish. The next day Mickey, Milt and fifteen of his cowhands went back to the place of the firefight and found the bodies where they lay but with their heads were crushed which was a typical Apache tactic.

Below are two pictures of Skeleton Canyon where Geronimo surrendered. These photos were found on the World Press Website.

Below is a close up photo of the exact place in Skeleton Canyon where Geronimo surrendered. The same trail that was followed by the escaping "Kid" and his gang. This Photo was also found on the Worldwide website

The men tried to follow the trail of the escaped Indians but with the water running in the creek their tracks were gone. According to Mickey's report to the local sheriff, the tracks they found indicated the Kid and his gang of renegade Apaches seemed to be heading back south toward Old Mexico through Skeleton Canyon.

Chapter Fifteen

In early 1899, Colonel Emilo Kosterlitzky, of the Mexican Ruales was in charge of the Mexican American Border. He was stationed in Nogales and went on record with Nogales reporter, stating "The Apache Kid" was alive and well, living in a village high in the Sierre Madre Mountains in the state of Chihuahua, Mexico. He said that he knew the location of the village where he lived with his family and he also stated that they were peaceful farmers and had been trading with the Mexicans for many years.

He went on to say that unlike the United States, Apaches that lived in peace in Mexico could stay there as long as they abided by the law and they lived in peace. He also said that Mexico had a different position with regard to peaceful Apaches. They were allowed to come and go as they pleased and that they did not believe in the reservation system that the United States adopted. He also said the Kid and his family know better than to mess with him because they know he was instrumental in the capture of Geronimo. I am going to go into the history of Colonel Kosterlizky because he is a very important piece of the puzzle with regard to the history of the life of the Kid after 1900.

On the next few pages are an article that was written by Samuel Truett that appeared in the Tucson Daily Star in May of 1961. The article covers the life of Emilio Kosterlizky;

A Mexican Cossack in Southern California

In August 1913, San Diego witnessed a strange sight. Trains bearing Mexican prisoners of war rolled into town, depositing their human cargo near the government barracks on Market Street. "Leather-lunged soldiers shouted weird military orders, and bewildered Mexican men and women chattered excitedly," wrote a reporter for the San Diego Sun. It was as if "some little Mexican town had been picked up with all its inhabitants and transplanted right here in San Diego."

It was a strange sight because the United States was not at war with Mexico. These men, women and children were refugees from border battles of the Mexican Revolution, raging since 1910. International law stipulated that the United States, a neutral neighbor was to hold them as prisoners of war until they could safely be returned to Mexico. They were bound for an interment camp at Fort Rosencrans, located just across San Diego Bay.

Stranger still was the bronzed man in a white sun helmet and a linen suit who towered over the other Mexicans. More than six feet tall, with thick glasses, he looked "more like a college professor or a scientist rather than a soldier." Another reporter wrote. The man before him was none other than Emilio Kosterlitzky, a legendary warrior whose career extended from the Apache Wars to the Mexican Revolution. Some called him a soldier of fortune, a world traveler in search of a good fight. Others said he was a Cossack who had traded the Russian steppes for Mexico. Like the enigmatic border hero of pulp fiction, he was a man without a history, a citizen without a nation.

What larger twist of fate brought this notorious warrior to California? His passage from Mexican battlefield to the United States interment camp evoked a familiar western plotline: a wild warrior caged, a lone rider unhorsed, the transformation of the wide-open frontier into a patrolled space between nations. Riding west into the sunset, Kosterlitzky prepared to vanish. "I have nothing to say that would make interesting reading," he told spectators. "I have been talked about enough in the papers. I want to be left out of them as much as possible from now on."

Border crossings were not new for Kosterlitzky. He was born in Moscow in 1853 as Emil Kosterlitzky, the child of a German mother and a Russian father.

His father was said to be a Cossack, a member of a military caste, usually composed of ethnic outsiders from Russia's frontiers who served as soldiers of the Tsarist state. Emil hoped to follow in his father's footsteps, but instead went into the navy. At 18 years of age, as a midshipman on a training vessel, he deserted off the Venezuela coast. "Still clinging to his love for horses and his ambition to become a cavalry leader," he sailed to the USA border and the state of Sonora, Mexico

- 164 -

and joined the Mexican army, changing his name to Emilio and set out to make a new start.

The borderlands offered expansive vistas for Kosterlizky. He became a Mexican by marrying into a Mexican family, but he also became part of a frontier military fraternity that gained status by fighting Indians in the 1880's, in the wars against the Apache Renegades and the Yaqui Indians, Kosterlizky became a defender of the nation's front lines. By brutally repressing one group, he earned his place as a citizen of another.

The Apache wars also opened doors north of the border. In 1882 as previously covered in another chapter of this book, Mexico and the United States signed a reciprocal crossing treaty, allowing troops to pursue renegade Apaches across each others borders. This law was presented by Kosterlizky and it helped him gain even more notoriety. In the 1880s, Kosterlitzky helped the U.S. soldiers in the Geronimo campaigns, and he later assisted in the suppression of such "bandits" as the Apache Kid, Nana and Massai. He was once described as "a favorite with all the boys in blue."

The U.S Army equated Kosterlitzky as the free and wild Cossack, a mythical icon not unlike the U.S. cowboy. The fact that he rode the Mexican countryside, not the Russian steppe, made him only more romantic. If the violence of the Frontier made

Kosterlitzky a citizen of a foreign land, the fantasy of the frontier ensured his rise as a local hero. His white skin and white horse set him apart from his brown-skinned neighbors, whom white American equated with banditry not heroism. In popular accounts, he was a picturesque leader, whereas his colleagues were considered rough characters.

Emilio Kosterlizky held his post as a Colonel of the Mexican Army until 1914 when because of his ability to speak over seven languages, became a member of the Mexican Secret Service. He has been on record in the Mexican newspaper, La Opinionas, saying he kept in touch with the Apache Kid until around 1905.

Below is a picture of Kosterlitzky taken circa 1913. From the National Archives.

There was another incident that was reported told by the Tombstone Epitaph that a local southern Arizona rancher by the name of Tom Charles, who insisted he was part of a posse led by a county sheriff, named Charles Anderson that supposedly trapped the Apache Kid on September 10th 1905 near Kingston in southwestern New Mexico and the posse shot him in a firefight. This story is probably not true, as nobody ever tried to claim the $5000 reward for the Kid dead or alive.

From time to time over the years the Kid made his way back to San Carlos to obtain new squaws. He was so feared by the Indians that lived at the San Carlos Reservation that his visits were only known after he had come and gone. He traveled with one or two squaws at all times. One would stay awake while he slept to watch guard and cook for him and the other would be his belly warmer. Then they would send the one he slept with out to stand guard and take the other one into his Wickieup. When the women were tired or worn out he would simply return to the reservation leave them and gather new traveling companions.

Did the Kid die in Mexico in 1910? Is a question that has haunted me since I took up this project. Was it really his spirit that appeared to me and the old medicine man? It was a lot of fun and I got a great buzz but reality, it is what it is, so to speak. I have been able to trace his life up to 1900 finding newspaper articles that support the fact that he was alive at the turn of the century.

Below and on the following page is an article that I found that was published in the Cleveland Weekly Plain Dealer on Friday January 23rd 1897. The article is priceless it demonstrates that the living legend, The Apache Kid's escapades were known from Arizona all the way back to Cleveland Ohio;

The Apache Kid

For seven years the meanest Indian in the southwest has been that very bad man known as the Apache Kid. The government says he has cost it $60,000 to keep watch of him at one time there have been necessary on both sides of the border, American and Mexican, as many as 400 soldiers trained to such business. In 1892 he rose to a sensation, and an issue, for our troops in New Mexico and Texas went for him in quite a campaign. The "Kid's" career has been as bloody as it has been pestiferous. The St. Louis Globe-Democrat says this of this mischievous outlaw:

"There has been a good deal written about the Apache Kid that is not true. The stories that have many believers are wild, weird tales, and except for the fact that the Apache Kid and his followers have committed many of the most dreadful murders and cruel thieveries on the border between the United States and Mexico, there is not one word of truth in them. The truth, as told among the reliable army officers and citizens who live adjacent to the San Carlos Indian reservation, who remember the villain well, and who have a dozen different photographs of the savage, is that he is a short, stocky, full blooded Apache.

He is wiry and bold, and has never had an hour's education in any government or private school. He never went out of Arizona until he became an outlaw, and never dressed in any garb of civilization, except the cast off clothing of people in Phoenix and Mesa, who took an interest in the lad some twelve or thirteen years ago, when he was best arrow and rifle shot on the San Carlos reservation. He is remembered by some of the non-commissioned officers in the United States army in the southwest as a participant in the numerous campaigns to capture the renegade Geronimo, when he was a sergeant of Indian scouts under General George Crook, and those who believe that the scouts didn't fool General Crook may also believe that Sergeant Kid rendered a valuable service in those campaigns.

He is skillful in Indian warfare, which is bushwacking; a dead shot at short range, like most Apaches; brave anywhere, except in the open and in the dark, where all of his tribe are cowards; and he has seen enough of the ways of troopers to be able to outwit and keep away from them.

In July, 1891, the Kid, with rare stealth, by night, traveled slowly down from the impenetrable fastness of the Gailuro Mountains, across the cactus desert in southern Arizona, northward to the Gila river country, where he hid for days on the outskirts of the San Carlos reservation. In some way he got word to a former girl companion of his, and she went out to visit the Kid in secret. He had ready an extra horse, stolen from a ranch nearby, and he forced her to flee with him back to the mountains. The girl, now twenty-four years of age was compelled by threats of instant death to live with the Kid and his gang for over a year.

She returned to the family wickieup on the reservation after suffering severe privations, and at the risk of her life. Hundreds of people in Phoenix and through the Gila River country knew her. The story she tells of the cruelty and devilish villainy of the Kid in the years of 1891 and 1892 is startling, and all of it has been proved true. According to the woman, several times, when preparations were made for the slaughter of a party of ranchmen or settlers that had been observed approaching the hiding place of the Kid and his gang in the mountain passes and canyons, she was tied to a tree and a bag put over her head so that she could neither escape or see in what direction the murderers had gone. Then a day or two later, when the savages saw that they were not followed by troops or avengers of the crime, the bloody intended party would stealthily return to free her and force her to accompany them to new scenes of robbery and murder.

One or two of her tales concerns the killing of women and children, who were always reserved until the last for putting to death, because they could do no harm to the savages, but they might tell some news to their slayers. Although the Indian girl could see nothing, the screaming appeals for their lives and for mercy at the hands of their bloodthirsty captors reached her ears as she was fastened to a tree.

As for the Kid himself, he is wandering along the border killing people once in awhile, and getting credit for a whole lot of devilry that drunken cowboys and Mexicans are guilty of. He has few companions, the fate of the rest of the band having made him wary of consorting with his own people too freely, and keeps out of the way of the troops that periodically go out to hunt for him. The Kid is not raiding for fun. He is a fugitive with a price on his head. Fifteen thousand dollars is the market value of his head, dead or alive, and he will kill rather than take chances of being caught. He is a literal Indian Ishmael. He has use for cartridges, provisions, money and sometimes for horses, and he takes what he wants. If the man who has what he wants is likely to object to giving it up, the Kid will kill him without a doubt.

A year ago last August, the Kid was identified on the Animas ranch, in the southern part of New Mexico. He was *getting away from troops at the time. A cattle ranchman drove a fine team right past the Kid's ambush, but was not molested. An hour later one of the ranchman's cowboys, who was hunting deer, had the bad luck to get in the Kid's way, in such a manner that the Kid could not avoid meeting him, and the Kid shot the cowboy.*

The recent international party of land surveyors, soldiers and laborers who went the full length of the border, from El Paso to San Diego, and established the boundary line, reports several reasons for believing the Kid was living (a year ago) in the mountains adjoining the Cocopah Indian Country on the east. He generally gave the party a wide berth, but they are sure he could not withstand the temptation to run off tow or three of their horses one night.

Below is an amazing article that was published Sunday April 16th 1950 in the Arizona Days and Ways section of the Arizona Republic. I believe this article clears up for all time the fate of the Apache Kid and the reason why the reward was never submitted or paid. It was written by Roscoe G. Willson, who was the foremost Arizona Historian of his time and author of five books;

The Story of Apache Kid's Gunfire Death Related

Virtually all writers on the subject of the Apache Kid have left his ultimate end in something of a haze, generally stating he supposedly died of disease in his Sierra Madre Mountain retreat.

This reasoning was due to the fact that one of the squaws, whom he had captured in Arizona and taken into Mexico, managed to escape and return to Arizona, bringing the report that the Kid was in poor health.

In refutation of the surmise the Kid died of disease, I have a statement by J. H. Webb of Vernon, Arizona, that the Kid, his squaw and her papoose were killed during an attempted robbery of a cornfield in the Mormon settlement of Cave Valley, Chihuahua, Mexico in the fall of 1900. Webb's story is substantiated by Dave Nelson, of Nelson Electric Company in Phoenix, who was living in the settlement at the time, and also by Carl Harris, whose uncle, Martin Harris and Tom Allen participated in the final chase and killing.

Webb's Story in his own words follows: In 1901 J. H. Webb went with his father to the Mormon settlement in Western Chihuahua, Mexico and in 1904, as a lad of 17 years, took employment at a sawmill operated by Dave Nelson's father, Hite Nelson, where Dave also was employed. Among his duties was the job of getting rid of the sawdust pile, which was set afire and slowly consumed. As the pile burned, pits and holes were created here and there and one day, to his surprised and consternation, he saw a human skull grinning up at him. He went into the mill and reported his find to the other workers. "Don't be scared, son," Hite Nelson told the excited boy.

"What you just saw was the skull of either the Apache Kid, or his squaw. The bones of the papoose are somewhere in that sawdust, too."

Nelson then told young Webb how the Apache Kid came to the end of his trail, and how his bones happened to be in the sawdust pile, substantially as follows:

In the year 1898 or 1999 the Kid, with a small band of followers, attached an outlying ranch and killed a Mrs. Thompson and her children. Pursuit by the armed ranchers and Mexican soldiers was unsuccessful, although the pursuers were close enough at times to sight the Kid at a distance.

About a year later, probably in the fall of 1900, Martin Harris and Thomas Allen, who had a ranch in Cave Valley, near the town of Pacheco, in Old Mexico, looked into their cornfield one night and discovered six or seven Indians stealing corn. Several shots were exchanged and the Indians ran off and disappeared in the darkness.

The next day Harris, Allen and several other ranchers took up the trail and followed it into the mountains. They were too late to catch the Indians in their night camp that day, but the following day surprised them in their noon camp.

Most of the Indians scattered like quail among the rocks, but the Kid and his squaw, with a papoose on her back, stood their ground. The Kid firing at his attackers until killed, supposedly by Harris or Martin. The squaw standing over her dead lover, seized the Kid's rifle and fired several shots before she was killed by a bullet, which also killed the papoose.

Both Harris and Allen upon examining the bodies found a .45 caliber old pistol that had been engraved with the name of Sheriff Glenn Reynolds of Gila County and had been stolen off the body of the dead Sheriff by the Apache Kid. Along with the pistol they found a gold watch that was also stolen off the body of Sheriff Reynolds by the Kid.

These two factors along with the dead Indian's likeness to the wanted poster and several neighbors who helped bury the trio in the cave on the mountainside assured them that they had in fact killed the notorious Apache Kid.

The killing was reported to the Mexican authorities, who in a few days came and exhumed the bodies, positively identifying the mail corpse as that of the Kid. The bodies were buried, and the settlers felt great satisfaction in knowing the notorious Apache Kid no longer would threaten their lives. The fact that from that time on the Mormon settlers had no more Indian trouble seemed sufficient proof the Kid indeed was dead.

A year or two later, when Thomas Allen was in El Paso on business, he met a doctor whom he related the story of the killing of the Apache Kid. The doctor was greatly interested, and for some reason wanted to obtain the *skeletons of the Kid and his family. He asked Allen if he would dig up the skeletons and bring them to El Paso.*

While the bones of he Kid were smoldering in the sawdust at Nelson's Mill Allen found out that, under Mexican Law, which assumed a person to be guilty until proven innocent, he might get himself into a peak of trouble if caught carrying human bones about with him; consequently, he wrote the doctor about the situation and promptly forgot the bones.

By the time the younger Webb discovered them a couple of years after the killing, they had become disintegrated, rotted and charred, and although he tried to save various pieces of bone as souvenirs of the Kid, they all crumbled in his hands.

Even though this author believes this is viable story of how the Apache Kid died. But because the story was passed down from Hite Nelson to J. H. Webb and then to Roscoe Willson, who was a very noted and trustworthy reporter, things get lost in translating from one person to another. The circumstances of the Kid's death. Bringing back a body from Mexico to the USA to be buried is not an easy chore. One does have to wonder though, since there was a $15,000 reward for him, dead or alive. If it really was the Kid's body, it is interesting that nobody tried to collect the reward for him.

One must consider the experience that the old medicine man and the author experienced.

Somehow there is evidence in this book indicating the whole experience we enjoyed together could possibly be true. The Kid could have lived out his life in Mexico and died in 1932, but sadly we will never have direct evidence of his death.

Most historians follow the Kid's life up to about 1891, then they conclude that he was either killed or died of Tuberculosis but none of them were able to substantiate a time and place of his death.

Newspaper articles are a historian's best friend. In some cases, yes there is biased reporting but for the most part these articles were written by people that were actually there at the time and serve as first hand information by trained and educated reporters, who in some cases are very accurate with their facts and dates. There is always a little redundancy with regard to newspaper articles but all in all they give us a first hand look at the facts surrounding historical events.

This author was able to find documentation of the Apache Kid's escapades well past 1891 with the newspaper articles that were found while the author spent many hours in the Phoenix Public Library, Sharlot Hall Museum in Prescott, The Arizona Historical Society Museum in Tempe, Arizona and finally the Arizona State Archives Museum in the State Capital Building here in Phoenix.

The bottom line is that the Apache Kid was no psychopath, but the last Native American who continued to wage a war up into the early 1900's.

A war that he knew he could never win. He was trying to protect his way of life and keep his land. He suffered from the "Coughing Sickness," as the Apaches called Tuberculosis and was addicted to pain medications. Not much different than folks today that are suffering from any incurable diseases.

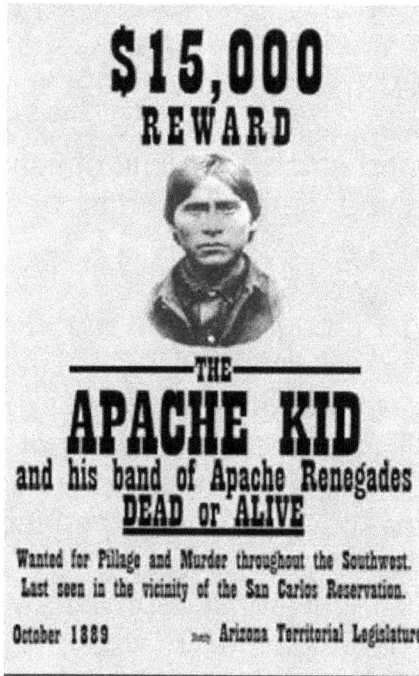

$15,000
REWARD

————THE————
APACHE KID
and his band of Apache Renegades
DEAD or ALIVE

Wanted for Pillage and Murder throughout the Southwest. Last seen in the vicinity of the San Carlos Reservation.

October 1889   Arizona Territorial Legislature

Above is a remake of the original wanted poster that was posted in every county sheriff's, town marshal's office, along with every bank and U.S. Post office in the territories of Arizona and New Mexico. Nobody has ever tried to collect on this reward. The Apache Kid simply disappeared and I believe he did die in Mexico. After Chief Eskiminzin was released from incarceration for helping the Kid. Eskiminzin also disappeared and supposedly was never seen again. I believe he and his family lived out their lives in the Sierra Madre Mountains in Sonora, Mexico.

In conclusion, as I rode away from the old medicine man's home, I realized thought I had been possibly scammed by the old man, in order for me to buy him the ingredients he needed to make another batch of Tiswin and pay his bar bill. back though, being a huge Depak Chopra disciple, I know that dealing with the spirit world is like going fishing. One day you can go to your favorite spot and catch your limit of fish. The next day at the same time and same place, catch nothing.

I must admit though, the old man and I had a wonderful time with that old man. I have gotten flash memory sparks on folks, in dealing with the spirit world all my life so that was not unusual. I wish I was fluent in the Apache language though, so it would have been a richer experience.

All in all, I received enough information with that old guy to guide me in writing this book. I have been able to find research to support everything the old man shared with me.

I was able to find research to support the Kid being alive after the turn of the century and that has been monumental because most historians believe he died in 1892. As always, I presented a lot of food for thought. I hope the reader enjoys this book as much as I did writing it.

Acknowledgements

William MacLeod Raine- Author- Famous Sheriffs
&Outlaws- Published by The New Home
Library- 1903

Phyllis De La Garza- Author- The Apache Kid
Western Lore Press- 1995

Bob Boze Bell- Author- Tragic Powwow-
True West Magazine-May 2006 Edition

Harry L. Payne- The Apache Kid- Informative
Article about the Kid found on the Internet

Ben T. Traywick- From Indian Scout to Southwest
Renegade- Article that appeared in the
August
2007 edition of the Tombstone Epitaph part of
a series of five articles written by Ben from
May through September of 2007

B. Ira Judd- The Apache Kid- An article that
published in the Arizona Highways Magazine
in the September issue in 1955

Darwin Van Campen- An article called
Hidden Canyon of the Aravaipa- published in
The August Issue of Arizona Highways

Shorty Finkenbinder- The failed Apache
Surrender
Conference- Article published in the February
2007 issue of the Tombstone Epitaph

Lucile and Charles W. Herbert- An article called
    Land of the San Carlos Apaches- published in
    Arizona Highways Magazine in the May 1963
Jay W. Sharp-Author- An article that appears in
    Desert USA- Profile of an Apache Woman

The Tucson Daily Star Newspaper for various
    articles that appeared over the years about
    The Apache Kid

The Phoenix City Herald Newspaper for various
    articles that appeared over the years about
    The Apache Kid

A Mexican Cossack written by Samuel Truett
    The Picture of Colonel Kosterlitzky courtesy
    of The University of Arizona Library

The Arizona Republic article in the Arizona Days
    and Ways section- Sunday April 16th 1950 by
    Their reporter Roscoe G. Willson called
    Simply the Story of Apache Kid's Gunfire
    Death Related

Arizona Album Section of the Arizona Republic
    article published on January 14, 1953 by
    reporter Albert R. Buehman titled Apache Kid
    Escaped 66 years ago in vicious battle with
    officers.

The Cleveland Weekly Plain Dealer newspaper,
    Friday January 22nd 1897 page 9, The
    "Apache Kid"

Wendy Goen ERM, Archivist and her staff at the
    Arizona State Archives

About the Author;

William "Tom" Vyles aka Zeke Crandall was born in London, Ontario, Canada. The family moved to Phoenix, Arizona in 1956. A life long battle with Asthma, several bouts with pneumonia, in an out of hospitals the first nine years of life, the family was instructed by physicians to move to Arizona for the hot dry climate.

In and out of school until age ten, home schooled by his mother Elizabeth, reading "The Books of Knowledge," encyclopedia, Tom fell in love with history. With no family in Arizona, our family adopted elderly neighbors, Kenny and Mary Harris, as our Arizona grandparents.

Kenny worked in the stockyards in Cincinnati as a brand inspector for cattle coming from Arizona. He became friends of John Wayne, who brought his cattle through the stockyards in Cincinnati. John talked Kenny into moving to Arizona. Kenny was a professional fiddle player, along with his friend Rudy MacDonald, who played banjo, they toured Arizona playing gigs.

Young Tom went along on most of the out of town music gigs. His job was to set up instruments and equipment. The carrot for Tom was that Kenny would take me rabbit and quail hunting the next day. Young Tom fell in love with Arizona history, because Kenny introduced him to many amazing older men, who told him stories of the old west.

For other books by this author, contact us by email, zekecrandall46@hotmail.com, FB Page-Tom Vyles or our website www.arizonatales.com. Look for new books to appear on Kindle on a three to four-month basis by this author. Thank You for your support.

www.ingramcontent.com/pod-product-compliance
Lightning Source LLC
Chambersburg PA
CBHW071437090426
42737CB00011B/1694